Presented To:

_____

FROM: _____

ON THE OCCASION OF: _____

DATE: _____

Luther's Morning Prayer

I thank You, my heavenly Father, through Jesus Christ, Your dear Son, that You have kept me this night from all harm and danger; and I pray that You would keep me this day also from sin and every evil, that all my doings and life may please You. For into Your hands I commend myself, my body and soul, and all things. Let Your holy angel be with me, that the evil foe may have no power over me. Amen.

Luther's Evening Prayer

I thank You, my heavenly Father, through Jesus Christ, Your dear Son, that You have graciously kept me this day; and I pray that You would forgive me all my sins where I have done wrong, and graciously keep me this night. For into Your hands I commend myself, my body and soul, and all things. Let Your holy angel be with me, that the evil foe may have no power over me. Amen.

LUTHER's
Small Catechism
for Kids

CONCORDIA PUBLISHING HOUSE • SAINT LOUIS

Table of Contents

Introduction

This is the Christian faith: grace freely given in Jesus. Out of His great mercy and love for us, God has done everything! On our own, we can do nothing good—but God is good, and God is love. This is the faith we desire to pass on to our children and to all children in our care: God the Father has given us *everything*—especially forgiveness and new life in Jesus Christ—and the Spirit leads us to respond with thankful love, trust, and devotion to God, as well as with love and service to our neighbor.

Martin Luther saw the need for a guide to teach people the basics of the Christian faith, rooted in God's Word. In 1529, Luther wrote the Small Catechism as a tool for teaching and learning the Christian faith and life. For centuries, it has been used at home, in schools, and in congregations.

Luther's Small Catechism for Kids uses age-appropriate, elementary-level language to explain and teach the basics of the faith to children ages 7–11. This resource was developed to help children learn and understand the foundational teachings of our faith and apply them to their lives. Because this resource is based on the text and structure of *Luther's Small Catechism with Explanation* (CPH, 2017), it will also provide a foundation for further study of the catechism.

However, this book is more than an instructional guide. It is a description of what it means to live as a baptized child of God, secure in His promise of unconditional love, forgiveness, and grace.

God bless you as you lead children through the catechism on an adventure of faith, discovering more about our great God and what it means to live as His beloved child.

Faith is a living, daring confidence in God's grace, so sure and certain that the believer would stake his life on it a thousand times.
—Martin Luther (AE 35:370)

How to Use This Book

Luther's Small Catechism for Kids loosely follows the structure and format of *Luther's Small Catechism with Explanation* (2017). While the explanation section has been rewritten in elementary-age language, the wording of the Six Chief Parts and Luther's explanation of them has been retained. Similarly, this catechism uses the English Standard Version translation of the Bible. This intentional alignment lays the foundation for further study of the catechism while helping to promote lifelong memorization of God's Word and our Christian beliefs.

The catechism is composed of Six Chief Parts: the Ten Commandments, the Creed, the Lord's Prayer, the Sacrament of Holy Baptism, Confession, and the Sacrament of the Altar.

The first half of the catechism examines the teaching of historically essential Christian texts: the Ten Commandments, the Creed, and the Lord's Prayer. Through the study of these texts, we learn how God calls us to repentance, faith, and new life in Christ.

The second half of the catechism describes how Christ is actively working in His Church through Baptism, Confession, and the Lord's Supper. The study of these sections clearly shows that Christ is with us to forgive us, renew us, and lead us, now and forever.

There are a variety of ways you can use this catechism to teach the faith.

The framework of the catechism makes it ideal for systematic teaching, one section at a time. You don't need to cover the material within a section all at once. Instead, pick and choose teaching points, questions, Bible illustrations, Scripture passages, and devotional content depending on the age, maturity, and interest of the children.

For example, when using this resource with **younger children**, you might read the main content with Luther's explanation, discuss the Main Idea, then move to the devotional content to connect learning to life.

Older children can dig deeper into the meaning of the main content by reading the bullet points and discussing one or more of the questions. They can also study Scripture passages and add more content as they mature.

Memorizing the chief parts of the catechism and Scripture verses is a wonderful way to instill the truth of God's Word in the heart.

Martin Luther never grew tired of studying the catechism. Although he was a learned preacher and teacher of the Word, he described himself as "a child" who studied and learned from the truth of the catechism daily. This is our prayer for you and the children with whom you share the faith!

Questions and Answers about the Christian Faith

What is the Christian faith?

The Christian faith is the belief that Jesus Christ is the only Savior of the world.

> **John 14:6** Jesus said to him, "I am the way, and the truth, and the life. No one comes to the Father except through Me."

Who is Jesus Christ?

Jesus is true God and true man in one person. He is the eternal Son of the Father, conceived by the Holy Spirit and born of the Virgin Mary to be our Savior and Lord.

> **John 17:3** This is eternal life, that they know You, the only true God, and Jesus Christ whom You have sent.

What has the one true God done?

God made all things and loves His creation, especially the people He created. From the time Adam and Eve sinned, every person has been born sinful, lives in sin, and faces death. God the Father sent His Son, Jesus, into the world to become man and to save all people by His death and resurrection. God sent His Spirit to bring people back to Him through faith in Jesus.

> **John 3:16** For God so loved the world, that He gave His only Son, that whoever believes in Him should not perish but have eternal life.

What is a Christian?

A Christian is a person who, by the power and work of the Holy Spirit through God's Word, believes in and confesses Jesus as Savior and Lord. Through Baptism, a Christian is adopted into God's family, the Church.

> **Romans 10:10** For with the heart one believes and is justified, and with the mouth one confesses and is saved.

What does it mean to confess (declare) Jesus Christ as my Lord?

To confess Jesus as my Lord means that I trust Him in life and in death as my Savior and my God. His death and resurrection have paid the punishment for all my sins and promise me eternal life. I belong to Jesus and I want to live for Him.

Romans 10:9, 13   If you confess with your mouth that Jesus is Lord and believe in your heart that God raised Him from the dead, you will be saved. . . . For "everyone who calls on the name of the Lord will be saved."

Where do we learn about Jesus?

We learn God's truth about Jesus Christ in the Bible. We call this truth the *Gospel* (the Good News), which is the promise of the forgiveness of sins for Jesus' sake. The Gospel is the main message of the Bible.

John 20:31   But these are written so that you may believe that Jesus is the Christ, the Son of God, and that by believing you may have life in His name.

What is the Bible?

The Bible is a collection of books written by prophets and apostles over a period of more than a thousand years. Through the Holy Spirit, God gave these writers the thoughts and words they wrote so that the Bible is God's Word. The Bible is completely true and has no mistakes. The Bible (Holy Scripture) tells us everything we need to know and believe for our Christian faith and life.

2 Timothy 3:16–17   All Scripture is breathed out by God and profitable for teaching, for reproof, for correction, and for training in righteousness, that the man of God may be complete, equipped for every good work.

Why can we be sure that the Bible is the true Word of God?

God's promises create faith in Jesus. Jesus tells us that all the Scriptures are God's own words and are completely true.

A. Jesus uses the Old Testament Scriptures as God's Word. He assures us that "Scripture cannot be broken" (John 10:35).

B. Jesus calls His own words true and says they are "spirit and life" (John 6:63).

C. Jesus gave others authority to speak His Word (see John 14:26).

What are the two great doctrines (teachings) of the Bible?

Law and Gospel are the two great doctrines of the Bible. The Law teaches what we are to do and not to do; the Gospel teaches what God has done, and still does, in Jesus for our salvation.

Romans 3:20   For by works of the law no human being will be justified in His sight, since through the law comes knowledge of sin.

Romans 1:16   For I am not ashamed of the gospel, for it is the power of God for salvation to everyone who believes, to the Jew first and also to the Greek.

Introduction to the Ten Commandments

The Ten Commandments are God's Law, His good and loving will for His beloved people.

- God's will for our lives is to love and trust Him more than anything or anyone else, and to love other people.
- God gave His Commandments because He loves us and He knows what is best for us.
- No one can keep the Commandments perfectly. We are all sinners. But God still loves us. Jesus, the Son of God, came to keep the Ten Commandments perfectly and then die on the cross to take the punishment for all our sins. Because of Jesus, we have forgiveness. God sent His Spirit to guide us and help us obey His commands.

You shall have no other gods.

What does this mean?
**We should fear, love, and trust
in God above all things.**

Understanding the First Commandment

THE MAIN IDEA
There is only
one true God.
God wants us to
put all our trust
in Him for every-
thing we need.

- We keep the First Commandment when we
  - respect God so much that we do nothing against His will;
  - love God more than anything and devote our life to Him; and
  - trust God will take care of all our needs and keep His promises to us.

- We sin against the First Commandment when we
  - worship any other god;
  - love or trust in anything or anyone more than God; or
  - make anything more important than God.

- The First Commandment summarizes all the Commandments. If we could love and honor God perfectly, we would be keeping all the other Commandments.

- No one can keep this or any of the Commandments perfectly. The Holy Spirit causes us to want to keep them, but we sometimes fail because we still have a sinful nature.

Learning about the First Commandment

What does it mean to have a god?

To have a god means to put our trust in someone or something to help us and give us all that we need.

Matthew 22:37–38 [Jesus] said to him, "You shall love the Lord your God with all your heart and with all your soul and with all your mind. This is the great and first commandment."

Why doesn't God want us to have any other gods besides Him?

God loves us. He knows He is the only one who can give us all we need for this life and for eternity.

Matthew 4:10   [Jesus said,] "You shall worship the Lord your God and Him only shall you serve."

What does it mean to fear God?

To fear God means to take God seriously. He is our Creator and Judge. He will judge the sinful world.

Proverbs 8:13   The fear of the LORD is hatred of evil.

What does it mean to trust and love God?

We trust and love God when we treasure Him more than anything else and rely on Him to take care of us and keep His promises to us.

Psalm 73:25   Whom have I in heaven but You? And there is nothing on earth that I desire besides You.

Who is the only true God?

The only true God is the triune God: Father, Son, and Holy Spirit. The Father reveals Himself in Jesus Christ. Jesus shows us the Father. The Father and the Son give us the Holy Spirit, who points to Jesus.

Matthew 28:19   Go therefore and make disciples of all nations, baptizing them in the name of the Father and of the Son and of the Holy Spirit.

A Bible Illustration

Jesus told a story about a man who put all his trust in his money and the things he owned. Read it in Luke 12:13–34.

Why was the rich man foolish?

Why should we put our trust in God instead of in earthly things or people?

Faith Connections

Think of one thing in this world you absolutely, positively could not live without. Is God more important than that thing (or person)? He should be!

God tells you, "Put Me first in your life." Why? Because He created you. He loves you. He is the only one who can help you with every single need you have in this life. God sent His Son, Jesus, to pay for your sinfulness and make you His child. He has given you the promise of eternal life. You can trust Him to keep His promises. When you sin and love other things more than God, you can turn to Him for forgiveness. Because Jesus died and rose, you are saved from your sins.

 ## Think and Share

What is God like? How can we describe Him? Look up some of these verses: Psalm 145:9; Isaiah 6:3; 1 John 4:8.

What are some of the things in this world that people put their trust in?

What are some of the ways God takes care of you every day? Make a list.

What's the most amazing thing God has done for you?

 ## Sing

I Am Trusting Thee, Lord Jesus (*LSB* 729:1, 4)

> I am trusting Thee, Lord Jesus, Trusting only Thee;
> Trusting Thee for full salvation, Great and free.

> I am trusting Thee to guide me; Thou alone shalt lead,
> Ev'ry day and hour supplying All my need.

 ## Bible Memory Verse

You shall love the LORD your God with all your heart and with all your soul and with all your might. (Deuteronomy 6:5)

 ## Pray

Dear God, thank You for all the ways You love and care for me. Help me to love and trust in You above all things. In Jesus' name I pray. Amen.

You shall not misuse the name of the LORD your God.

What does this mean?
We should fear and love God so that we do not curse, swear, use satanic arts, lie, or deceive by His name, but call upon it in every trouble, pray, praise, and give thanks.

Understanding the Second Commandment

- We keep the Second Commandment when we
  - talk to God in prayer, asking good for ourselves and others;
  - call on God in times of trouble;
  - thank and praise Him for His blessings; and
  - speak truthfully about God according to His Word.

- We sin against the Second Commandment when we
  - *swear* (call on God to witness the truth of what we say) thoughtlessly;
  - curse by using God's name in a disrespectful way; or
  - use God's name as a magic charm, to curse others, or to do things that are against His will.

> **THE MAIN IDEA**
> When we love and trust God as our Creator, Savior, and Helper, God's names are special to us.

Learning about the Second Commandment

What is God's name?

God's name is every name that He has used to make Himself known. In the Old Testament, we learn God's personal name: *Yahweh*, which means "I am." In the New Testament, we learn a new personal name: *Jesus*, which means "Yahweh saves."

Exodus 3:13–14 "[If] they ask me, 'What is His name?' what shall I say to them?" God said to Moses, "I AM WHO I AM." And He said, "Say this to the people of Israel: 'I AM has sent me to you.'"

Matthew 1:21 She will bear a son, and you shall call His name Jesus, for He will save His people from their sins.

Why did God give us His name?

God gave us His name so we could know who created us and redeems and guides us—so that we could call on Him in prayer and so that we could tell others about Him.

Luke 11:2   [Jesus] said to them, "When you pray, say: 'Father, hallowed be Your name.'"

Isaiah 44:24   Thus says the LORD, your Redeemer, who formed you from the womb: "I am the LORD, who made all things, who alone stretched out the heavens, who spread out the earth by Myself."

John 14:26   But the Helper, the Holy Spirit, whom the Father will send in My name, He will teach you all things and bring to your remembrance all that I have said to you.

What are some wrong ways to use God's name?

We misuse God's name when we speak badly about God, say things about Him that are untrue, use swear words or curse words, and talk about God in a way that does not honor Him.

Leviticus 19:12   You shall not swear by My name falsely, and so profane the name of your God: I am the LORD.

A Bible Illustration

When Mary learned she would become the mother of the promised Savior, she sang a song of thanks and praise that we call the *Magnificat* (a Latin word meaning "praise"). Read it in Luke 1:39–56.

What names of God did Mary sing?

How does Mary describe what God has done for her and all people?

Faith Connections

Think about the names or titles that you use when you talk to those who care for you: your parents and caregivers, your teacher, your pastor, your doctor. How do those names and titles show respect and love?

God is our Creator, Savior, and Helper, the one who will always love, forgive, and care for us. When we call on God using the names He has given to us in His Word, the Bible, we show Him love, respect, and thankfulness for all that He has done for us.

 ## Think and Share

Give an example of how someone might use God's name disrespectfully. Give an example of using God's name in a good way.

What are some of your favorite names of God from the Bible? What makes them so special to you?

Write your own prayer or song to God, describing who He is and what He has done for you. Then pray it or teach it to your family to sing together.

 ## Sing

How Sweet the Name of Jesus Sounds (*LSB* 524:1, 4)

> How sweet the name of Jesus sounds In a believer's ear!
> It soothes our sorrows, heals our wounds, And drives away our fear.
>
> O Jesus, shepherd, guardian, friend, My Prophet, Priest, and King,
> My Lord, my life, my way, my end, Accept the praise I bring.

 ## Bible Memory Verse

> Call upon Me in the day of trouble; I will deliver you, and you shall glorify Me. (Psalm 50:15)

 ## Pray

Dear heavenly Father, Your name is holy! Keep me from using Your name in any way that would dishonor You. Let Your Holy Spirit help me to honor Your name in everything that I think, do, and say. In Jesus' name I pray. Amen.

Remember the Sabbath day by keeping it holy.

What does this mean?
We should fear and love God so that we do not despise preaching and His Word, but hold it sacred and gladly hear and learn it.

Understanding the Third Commandment

- We keep the Third Commandment when we
  - treasure God's Word as sacred; and
  - take time to hear and learn His Word at home and in public worship.

- We sin against the Third Commandment when we
  - do not attend church to receive God's Word and the blessing of His Sacraments; or
  - do not read or listen to God's Word.

> **THE MAIN IDEA**
> God strengthens our faith in Him when we hear His Word and receive His blessings.

Learning about the Third Commandment

What is the Sabbath day?

In the Old Testament, God set apart the seventh day (Saturday) as a day of rest for His people to worship Him and to remember all He had done for them.

Exodus 20:8–11   Remember the Sabbath day, to keep it holy. Six days you shall labor, and do all your work, but the seventh day is a Sabbath to the LORD your God. On it you shall not do any work, you, or your son, or your daughter, your male servant, or your female servant, or your livestock, or the sojourner who is within your gates. For in six days the LORD made heaven and earth, the sea, and all that is in them, and rested on the seventh day. Therefore the LORD blessed the Sabbath day and made it holy.

Why do Christians today no longer observe the Sabbath day (Saturday) as the Old Testament Israelite people did?

The Sabbath was a sign pointing to Jesus, who gives us spiritual rest from our sins. In the New Testament, Christians began worshiping God on Sunday, the day Jesus rose from the dead (see also Colossians 2:16–17).

Matthew 12:8 The Son of Man is lord of the Sabbath.

Matthew 11:28 [Jesus said,] "Come to Me, all who labor and are heavy laden, and I will give you rest."

How do God's people today keep the Sabbath day?

Christians today set aside time to worship God, hear His Word, and focus on all that God has done for us. We also celebrate the seasons and holy days of the Church Year.

Colossians 3:16 Let the word of Christ dwell in you richly, teaching and admonishing one another in all wisdom, singing psalms and hymns and spiritual songs, with thankfulness in your hearts to God.

Why is it important for God's people to gather together with other Christians in public worship?

God is with us as His Word is preached and His Sacraments of Baptism and the Lord's Supper are given, and we receive His forgiveness. Christians encourage one another in the faith as we sing and pray together.

Hebrews 10:24–25 Let us consider how to stir up one another to love and good works, not neglecting to meet together, as is the habit of some, but encouraging one another, and all the more as you see the Day drawing near.

A Bible Illustration

When Jesus visited the home of His friends Mary and Martha, He praised the actions of one of the women more than the other. Read it in Luke 10:38–42.

Why did Jesus praise Mary for listening to Him?

What is the "one thing necessary" that Mary chose?

Faith Connections

Is there a favorite place you like to go because you know you'll get something special when you get there? Maybe it's Grandma's house, where there are always chocolate chip cookies waiting for you. Maybe it's school or basketball, where your friends greet you with high-fives.

King David had a favorite place to go—God's house! David wrote, "O LORD, I love the habitation of Your house and the place where Your glory dwells" (Psalm 26:8). Why did David love to go to God's house? What did he get there? The same things we receive: God's forgiveness and love and the strengthening of our faith.

 ## Think and Share

Why does God want us to set aside a time to rest and worship Him?

What are some excuses we and others have for not going to church or reading His Word?

What gifts does God give us in the worship service?

How does God's Word open our eyes to see all that He has done for us?

 ## Sing

Blessed Jesus, at Your Word (*LSB* 904:1)

    Blessed Jesus, at Your Word We are gathered all to hear You.
    Let our hearts and souls be stirred Now to seek and love and fear You,
    By Your teachings, sweet and holy, Drawn from earth to love You solely.

 ## Bible Memory Verse

O LORD, I love the habitation of Your house and the place where Your glory dwells. (Psalm 26:8)

 ## Pray

Dear Lord Jesus, You promised that everyone who hears Your Word and obeys will be blessed. Help me set aside time to study Your Word and to worship You. Help me say, "I love the habitation of Your house!" In Your name I pray. Amen.

Honor your father and your mother.

What does this mean?
We should fear and love God so that we do not despise or anger our parents and other authorities, but honor them, serve and obey them, love and cherish them.

Understanding the Fourth Commandment

- We keep the Fourth Commandment when we
  - recognize that parents, guardians, and other authorities are God's representatives who serve in His place to care for us;
  - love, honor, serve, and help our parents, guardians, and other authorities; and
  - obey our parents, guardians, pastors, teachers, employers, government authorities, and all those God has placed in authority over us.

> **THE MAIN IDEA**
> We love, honor, and respect our parents as God's gifts to us and His representatives on earth.

- We sin against the Fourth Commandment when we
  - look down on or make fun of parents and other authorities; or
  - hurt or refuse to obey parents and others who have authority over us.

Learning about the Fourth Commandment

Why must we honor parents, guardians, and others who have authority over us?

God gave parents, guardians, and other authorities to serve in His place, as His representatives, to care for us.

Colossians 3:20 Children, obey your parents in everything, for this pleases the Lord.

Romans 13:1 Let every person be subject to the governing authorities. For there is no authority except from God, and those that exist have been instituted by God.

What kind of relationship does God want us to have with our parents, guardians, and others in authority over us?

God wants us to honor and serve one another as Jesus has loved us, and to do all that we can to bring one another happiness.

John 13:34 [Jesus said,] "A new commandment I give to you, that you love one another: just as I have loved you, you also are to love one another."

What promise does God give with this commandment, and why does He give it?

God promises that when you honor your parents, it will "go well with you" and you will "live long in the land." This promise shows the importance of parents raising children to be caretakers of God's creation, who share the Gospel of Jesus.

Ephesians 6:1–3 Children, obey your parents in the Lord, for this is right. "Honor your father and mother" (this is the first commandment with a promise), "that it may go well with you and that you may live long in the land."

Is there ever a time when we must disobey our parents or others in authority?

We must disobey them if they tell us to do something that is against God's will or His Word.

Acts 5:29 We must obey God rather than men.

A Bible Illustration

Jesus showed love and honor to His mother, even as He was dying on the cross. Read about it in John 19:25–27.

How did Jesus show love and honor to His mother in this passage?

How did John show honor to Jesus' mother?

Faith Connections

Who takes care of you when you are sick? Who gives you food to eat and buys you clothes and toys? Who helps you with homework? God gives you parents, guardians, teachers, and others to take care of you, guide you, and teach you about Him.

God made you and He continues to care for you. One of the ways He takes care of you is by giving you parents and others to love, guide, and teach you.

 ## Think and Share

What are some ways that you can show love and honor to your parents and others who care for you?

What can you do this week to thank your parents and others in authority over you?

Give an example of a time when you should not obey what your parents or others tell you to do. Explain why you would need to disobey them in that situation.

How does obeying your parents, guardians, and others in authority help to keep good order in the world?

 ## Sing

These Are the Holy Ten Commands (*LSB* 581:5; *OAR* 352:5)
> "You are to honor and obey Your father, mother, ev'ry day,
> Serve them each way that comes to hand;
> You'll then live long in the land." Have mercy, Lord!

 ## Bible Memory Verse

Children, obey your parents in everything, for this pleases the Lord. (Colossians 3:20)

 ## Pray

Dear God, thank You for the gift of those who care for me! Help me to love and obey them, and bless my family with Your love. In Jesus' name I pray. Amen.

You shall not murder.

What does this mean?
**We should fear and love God so that we do not
hurt or harm our neighbor in his body, but help
and support him in every physical need.**

Understanding the Fifth Commandment

- We keep the Fifth Commandment when we
  - help other people in need;
  - defend people who are falsely accused; and
  - treat other people with kindness and compassion.

- We sin against the Fifth Commandment when we
  - hurt or kill another person;
  - do or say something that puts someone's life in danger;
  - refuse to help someone in need; or
  - hate another person.

> **THE MAIN IDEA**
> God made us to care
> about other people
> and to help them in
> times of need so they
> can enjoy the life
> God has given them.

Learning about the Fifth Commandment

Who is our neighbor?

Every person God has created is our neighbor, especially those who need our help. "Our neighbor" includes people of every race and ethnicity.

Matthew 22:39 You shall love your neighbor as yourself.

How do we commit murder in our heart?

We commit murder in our heart when we hate another person. We hurt others when we make them angry or unhappy by saying or doing mean things to them.

1 John 4:20–21 If anyone says, "I love God," and hates his brother, he is a liar; for he who does not love his brother whom he has seen cannot love God whom he has not seen. And this commandment we have from Him: whoever loves God must also love his brother.

What are some ways we are to help and defend our neighbor?

We are to help our neighbor with physical needs, such as hunger or protection; speak in a way that defends our neighbor from wrongdoing; and treat our neighbor with kindness and compassion.

Romans 12:20   If your enemy is hungry, feed him; if he is thirsty, give him something to drink.

Proverbs 31:8–9   Open your mouth for the mute, for the rights of all who are destitute. Open your mouth, judge righteously, defend the rights of the poor and needy.

Ephesians 4:32   Be kind to one another, tenderhearted, forgiving one another, as God in Christ forgave you.

What does the Fifth Commandment say about life issues in our society today?

God creates, cares for, and protects all life. He wants us to care for and protect all that He has created, especially human life. Every human life is precious to God and to all Christians. This commandment forbids ending the life of others—including an unborn child—or oneself, or helping someone to end his or her own life.

Genesis 1:27   God created man in His own image, in the image of God He created him; male and female He created them.

Psalm 139:16   Your eyes saw my unformed substance; in Your book were written, every one of them, the days that were formed for me, when as yet there was none of them.

1 Corinthians 3:16–17   Do you not know that you are God's temple and that God's Spirit dwells in you? If anyone destroys God's temple, God will destroy him. For God's temple is holy, and you are that temple.

A Bible Illustration

Jesus told a story about a man who helped his neighbor in need. Read it in Luke 10:25–37.

How did the priest and the Levite sin against the Fifth Commandment?

How did the Samaritan keep the Fifth Commandment?

Faith Connections

Here are some amazing facts about the human body: The human heart will beat more than three billion times in an average lifetime. Human teeth are just as strong as shark teeth. The human nose can recognize a trillion different scents. Laid end to end, an adult's blood vessels could circle the earth's equator four times. God made all humans amazingly complex and wonderful—including you!

But even more wonderful is how much God loves and cares for you and all people—so much that He sent His Son, Jesus, to die for your sins and for the sins of all people. God calls you to love others as He has loved you. "We love because He first loved us" (1 John 4:19).

 ## Think and Share

Who is our neighbor? Is there anyone who is not our neighbor?

How should we act toward people who have been unkind to us? How are we able to show kindness, even to our enemies?

Why is every human life important and precious to God and to all Christians?

 ## Sing

O God of Mercy, God of Might (*LSB* 852:3, 5)
> Teach us the lesson Thou has taught: To feel for those Thy blood hath bought,
> That ev'ry word and deed and thought May work a work for Thee.

> In sickness, sorrow, want, or care, May we each other's burdens share;
> May we, where help is needed, there Give help as unto Thee!

 ## Bible Memory Verse

> Be kind to one another, tenderhearted, forgiving one another, as God in Christ forgave you. (Ephesians 4:32)

 ## Pray

Dear God, take away all my anger and hatred toward other people. Help me to be kind and forgiving, willing to help others and love them as You love me. In Jesus' name I pray. Amen.

You shall not commit adultery.

What does this mean?
We should fear and love God so that we lead a sexually pure and decent life in what we say and do, and husband and wife love and honor each other.

Understanding the Sixth Commandment

- We keep the Sixth Commandment when we
  - respect God's purpose for marriage by saving sexual activity for marriage;
  - resist the temptation of sinful sexual desires and activities;
  - speak and act respectfully to one another as male and female; and
  - respect and cherish marriage as the lifelong union of a man and a woman.

> **THE MAIN IDEA**
> God created us male and female. God's will is for us to lead a sexually pure life and to cherish marriage as the lifelong union of a man and a woman.

- We sin against the Sixth Commandment when we
  - engage in sexual activities outside of marriage;
  - look at or engage in impure thoughts and activities; or
  - use impure language or treat our bodies or others' bodies disrespectfully.

Learning about the Sixth Commandment

What is marriage?

Marriage is the lifelong union of a man and a woman.

Mark 10:6–9   But from the beginning of creation, "God made them male and female." "Therefore a man shall leave his father and mother and hold fast to his wife, and the two shall become one flesh." So they are no longer two but one flesh. What therefore God has joined together, let not man separate.

What is adultery?

Adultery is when a person desires or has sexual relations with someone to whom he or she is not married.

Hebrews 13:4   Let marriage be held in honor among all, and let the marriage bed be undefiled, for God will judge the sexually immoral and adulterous.

Does this commandment apply only to husbands and wives?

No, the command to lead a sexually pure life is for all people, both married and unmarried, and it applies to all kinds of sexual desire and activity.

Matthew 5:27–28   You have heard that it was said, "You shall not commit adultery." But I say to you that everyone who looks at a woman with lustful intent has already committed adultery with her in his heart.

What does the Bible say about same-sex marriage?

God created us as male and female and created marriage as the lifelong union between a man and a woman. Same-sex marriage is against God's will and is not true marriage.

Romans 1:26–27   For their women exchanged natural relations for those that are contrary to nature; and the men likewise gave up natural relations with women and were consumed with passion for one another, men committing shameless acts with men and receiving in themselves the due penalty for their error.

What does the Bible say about divorce and remarriage?

Divorce is against God's will except in cases of unfaithfulness or abuse. The Bible allows for divorce and remarriage in those circumstances.

Matthew 19:9   [Jesus said,] "I say to you: whoever divorces his wife, except for sexual immorality, and marries another, commits adultery."

A Bible Illustration

God created man and woman to help and bring joy to each other as they live their lives together in marriage. Read about it in Genesis 2:15–24.

Why did God create Eve?

How does this Bible passage show God's will for marriage?

Faith Connections

What is God's most amazing creation? You! God knew everything about you before you were born—whether you would be a boy or girl, the color of your eyes, and the number of hairs on your head. Nothing about you is a mistake—you are wonderfully made! Most important, God chose you to be His precious child. You and the body God gave you are special gifts. God wants you to care for and respect your body; He wants you to respect other people too. "Do you not know that your body is a temple of the Holy Spirit within you, whom you have from God? You are not your own, for you were bought with a price. So glorify God in your body" (1 Corinthians 6:19–20).

 ## Think and Share

How has God made you special? How can you care for and respect your body?

What is God's will for marriage?

What can help you lead a pure and God-pleasing life?

 ## Sing

Renew Me, O Eternal Light (*LSB* 704:2–3)

> Remove the pow'r of sin from me And cleanse all my impurity
> That I may have the strength and will Temptations of the flesh to still.

> Create in me a new heart, Lord, That gladly I obey Your Word.
> Let what You will be my desire, And with new life my soul inspire.

 ## Bible Memory Verse

Create in me a clean heart, O God, and renew a right spirit within me.
(Psalm 51:10)

 ## Pray

Dear God, help me remember that You have made me special and that You live in me. Take away all impure thoughts and desires, and help me respect others and myself. Give me strength to resist what is wrong and to do what is right in Your eyes. In Jesus' name I pray. Amen.

You shall not steal.

What does this mean?

We should fear and love God so that we do not take our neighbor's money or possessions, or get them in any dishonest way, but help him to improve and protect his possessions and income.

Understanding the Seventh Commandment

- We keep the Seventh Commandment when we
  - protect and improve our neighbor's possessions;
  - return items that are not ours to their rightful owners; and
  - provide for those who are in need.

- We sin against the Seventh Commandment when we
  - steal our neighbor's possessions or money;
  - get things dishonestly or take advantage of others; or
  - damage things that belong to others.

> **THE MAIN IDEA**
> God wants us to protect and care for the things that belong to our neighbor.

Learning about the Seventh Commandment

Why are earthly goods such as money and possessions important?

Money and possessions are gifts from God, which God has given to us to provide for our needs, to enjoy, and to use to help others.

2 Corinthians 9:8–10 And God is able to make all grace abound to you, so that having all sufficiency in all things at all times, you may abound in every good work. As it is written, "He has distributed freely, He has given to the poor; His righteousness endures forever." He who supplies seed to the sower and bread for food will supply and multiply your seed for sowing and increase the harvest of your righteousness.

What does it mean to steal from our neighbor?

Stealing includes taking something that does not belong to us; cheating or taking advantage of someone; not paying back debts; not doing an honest day's work; and illegally playing or copying items such as music, software, movies, and personal information from online or digital sources.

Ephesians 4:28   Let the thief no longer steal, but rather let him labor, doing honest work with his own hands, so that he may have something to share with anyone in need.

Psalm 37:21   The wicked borrows but does not pay back, but the righteous is generous and gives.

Why is damaging our neighbor's property a form of stealing?

When something is damaged, its value and usefulness are reduced so that the person is not able to use it. Damaging items is stealing their usefulness.

Philippians 2:4   Let each of you look not only to his own interests, but also to the interests of others.

How should we use the earthly goods that God has given to us?

God has given us earthly goods to provide for our own families, to help others who are in need, and to give to the Church so the Good News can be proclaimed and shared.

1 John 3:17   But if anyone has the world's goods and sees his brother in need, yet closes his heart against him, how does God's love abide in him?

Hebrews 13:16   Do not neglect to do good and to share what you have, for such sacrifices are pleasing to God.

A Bible Illustration

Jesus changed the heart of Zacchaeus from greedy to generous. Read about it in Luke 19:1–10.

What changed Zacchaeus's heart?

What proof do you see of the change in Zacchaeus?

Faith Connections

Take a look around you. Can you name five things that God has given to you? Can you name more?

God loves to bless us with good things—just look at the beautiful earth that He made for us! God wants us to share the things He has given us with others. Think of someone who might be in need of food or clothes or other earthly items. How could you help them? Make a plan this week to share some of God's gifts to you with others.

 ## Think and Share

What types of things do people steal from others?

What are some other ways that people steal?

What should we do if we find something that is not ours?

How can you help someone in need this week?

 ## Sing

Son of God, Eternal Savior (*LSB* 842:2)
> As You, Lord, have lived for others, So may we for others live.
> Freely have Your gifts been granted; Freely may Your servants give.
> Yours the gold and Yours the silver, Yours the wealth of land and sea;
> We but stewards of Your bounty Held in solemn trust will be.

 ## Bible Memory Verse

> Do not neglect to do good and to share what you have, for such sacrifices are pleasing to God. (Hebrews 13:16)

 ## Pray

Dear God, forgive me for times I have taken what is not mine. Give me a loving heart to share what You have given me to help those who are in need. In Jesus' name I pray. Amen.

You shall not give false testimony against your neighbor.

What does this mean?
We should fear and love God so that we do not tell lies about our neighbor, betray him, slander him, or hurt his reputation, but defend him, speak well of him, and explain everything in the kindest way.

Understanding the Eighth Commandment

- We keep the Eighth Commandment when we
  - defend our neighbors if others speak badly of them;
  - point out people's good qualities and actions; and
  - try to understand the actions of others in the most positive light and explain them in the kindest way.

- We sin against the Eighth Commandment when we
  - tell lies about people;
  - betray others by sharing their secrets or faults; or
  - spread rumors or complain about others.

> **THE MAIN IDEA**
> God wants us to speak truthful and kind words about our neighbors so that others will think well of them.

Learning about the Eighth Commandment

Why is a good reputation (the way others think about you) important?

It is important to have a good name or reputation so that we can enjoy the trust and respect of others.

Proverbs 22:1   A good name is to be chosen rather than great riches, and favor is better than silver or gold.

What are some ways that people's reputations are hurt or destroyed?

People's reputations are damaged when we make fun of them, gossip about them, bully them in person or on social media, exclude them, or pit others against them.

James 4:11   Do not speak evil against one another, brothers.

Proverbs 11:13 Whoever goes about slandering reveals secrets, but he who is trustworthy in spirit keeps a thing covered.

What should we do to protect our neighbor's good name?

We should defend our neighbor against lies and say good things about our neighbor whenever we can. When we hear something about our neighbor that we don't know is true, we should try to understand the situation in the most positive way and speak of the person in the kindest way.

Proverbs 31:8–9 Open your mouth for the mute, for the rights of all who are destitute. Open your mouth, judge righteously, defend the rights of the poor and needy.

The Bible tells us to speak the truth in love (Ephesians 4:15). What does this mean?

We are to speak the truth of God's Word to others, gently pointing out the dangers of false teachings.

Ephesians 4:15 Rather, speaking the truth in love, we are to grow up in every way into Him who is the head, into Christ.

1 Thessalonians 5:14 And we urge you, brothers, admonish the idle, encourage the fainthearted, help the weak, be patient with them all.

A Bible Illustration

Jesus praised and defended the woman who anointed Him when others were speaking poorly of her. Read about it in Mark 14:3–9.

What were people saying against the woman?

How did Jesus defend her and speak well of her?

Faith Connections

"Sticks and stones may break my bones, but names will never hurt me!" That saying isn't true, is it? Names and unkind words, gossip and rumors do hurt people, sometimes even more than a stick or a stone. We know how deeply an unkind word can hurt. We also know how a kind word can make someone happy and thankful. God wants our words and actions toward others to be kind and loving, just as He is kind and loving toward each of us, His children. This week, think about your words before you say them. Try to build someone up instead of tearing him or her down. It will make both of you happy!

 ## Think and Share

What can you do when others are saying unkind words about someone?

How could you help stop a rumor from spreading?

Think of someone who has not been treated nicely. What could you do to build that person up?

When might you need to "speak the truth in love" to someone?

 ## Sing

O God, My Faithful God (*LSB* 696:3)
> Keep me from saying words That later need recalling;
> Guard me lest idle speech May from my lips be falling;
> But when within my place I must and ought to speak,
> Then to my words give grace Lest I offend the weak.

 ## Bible Memory Verse

Above all, keep loving one another earnestly, since love covers a multitude of sins. (1 Peter 4:8)

 ## Pray

Dear God, help me to guard my tongue so that I don't say unkind or untrue words. Fill my heart with the love of Christ so that I always say things that are helpful and true. In Jesus' name I pray. Amen.

You shall not covet your neighbor's house.

What does this mean?
We should fear and love God so that we do not
scheme to get our neighbor's inheritance or house,
or get it in a way which only appears right, but
help and be of service to him in keeping it.

You shall not covet your neighbor's wife, or his manservant or maidservant, his ox or donkey, or anything that belongs to your neighbor.

What does this mean?
We should fear and love God so that we do not entice or force
away our neighbor's wife, workers, or animals, or turn them
against him, but urge them to stay and do their duty.

Understanding the Ninth and Tenth Commandments

- We keep the Ninth and Tenth Commandments
  when we
  ○ are thankful for all that God has given us; and
  ○ help others keep what God has given them.

- We sin against the Ninth and Tenth Commandments when we
  ○ are not grateful for the things we have;
  ○ try to get other people's property by tricking or
    deceiving them; or
  ○ try to take away our neighbor's friends or turn them against him.

> **THE MAIN IDEA**
> God wants us to be
> content (happy and
> satisfied) with the gifts
> that He has given to
> us and not try to get
> what is not ours.

Learning about the Ninth and Tenth Commandments

What is coveting?

Coveting is a sinful desire in our heart to have or to take away something that belongs to someone else.

James 4:2   You desire and do not have, so you murder. You covet and cannot obtain, so you fight and quarrel. You do not have, because you do not ask.

How are we tempted to be unsatisfied with what we have?

We compare ourselves with others and desire what they have, thinking that things will make us happy. We do not trust that God will give us all we need.

Hebrews 13:5   Keep your life free from love of money, and be content with what you have, for [God] has said, "I will never leave you nor forsake you."

Is all wanting of earthly things sinful?

No. God encourages us to look to Him for blessings of food, shelter, good jobs, health, and other things that will help ourselves and our family.

Philippians 4:6   Do not be anxious about anything, but in everything by prayer and supplication with thanksgiving let your requests be made known to God.

How does God want us to feel about things that belong to our neighbor?

God wants us to be happy when our neighbor does well, and He wants us to do all that we can to help our neighbor keep his or her property.

Philippians 2:4   Let each of you look not only to his own interests, but also to the interests of others.

A Bible Illustration

King Ahab wanted Naboth's property. Wicked Queen Jezebel came up with a plan to kill Naboth so Ahab could have it. Read about it in 1 Kings 21:1–16.

How did Ahab react when Naboth wouldn't sell his vineyard?

What commandments did Jezebel break to get the vineyard for Ahab?

Faith Connections

It's sometimes hard to be content with what we have, isn't it? We look around and see our friends with the latest phone, expensive shoes, or new clothes, and we start thinking, "If only I could have _____, then I would be happy." But getting everything we want doesn't give us true happiness and contentment. It often just makes us want even more! God knows that we will only truly be happy when we look to Him for all our needs and give thanks for all that He has given us. He gives us much more than we could ever need, especially life and forgiveness in the death and resurrection of Jesus!

 ## Think and Share

Make a list of all the blessings God has given you—then thank Him for them!

Is it okay to want something you don't have? When does wanting something become a sin?

It's not only physical things we covet. We might covet other people's beauty, talents, or abilities. What can happen when we want things that belong to other people?

 ## Sing

What Is the World to Me (*LSB* 730:3)
>   The world seeks after wealth And all that mammon offers
>   Yet never is content Though gold should fill its coffers.
>   I have a higher good, Content with it I'll be:
>   My Jesus is my wealth. What is the world to me!

 ## Bible Memory Verse

   Be content with what you have. (Hebrews 13:5)

 ## Pray

   Dear God, please forgive me for the times that I want what You have given to others. Help me to be happy and content with all that You give to me, and help me to look to You for everything I need. In Jesus' name I pray. Amen.

Introduction to the Apostles' Creed

The Apostles' Creed tells us the most important truths about God: who He is and what He has done. God is the Father, Son, and Holy Spirit—the Holy Trinity. The Creed's three parts tell about the divine work of each person of the Trinity: the Father (creation), the Son (redemption), and the Holy Spirit (sanctification).

- A creed is a statement of what we believe, teach, and confess to be true.
- The Apostles' Creed is a summary of what the Bible teaches us about God.
- The Apostles' Creed teaches us about the one true God: Father, Son, and Holy Spirit—the Trinity.

I believe in God, the Father Almighty, Maker of heaven and earth.

What does this mean?
I believe that God has made me and all creatures; that He has given me my body and soul, eyes, ears, and all my members, my reason and all my senses, and still takes care of them.

Understanding the First Article (Part 1): Creation

- God the Father is our Father and the Father of Jesus Christ, the Son of God.
- God created all things in six days by the power of His Word.
- Humans are God's greatest creation.
- God created angels to be His messengers and to serve Him.

> **THE MAIN IDEA**
> I believe that God created the world and all things: the things we can see, and the things we cannot see. God also created me. Humans are God's greatest creation!

Learning about the First Article (Part 1): Creation

Why is the First Person of the Trinity called God the Father?

- He is the Father of the Son of God, Jesus, our Savior. (But Jesus was always there, from the beginning.)
- He is the Father of all Christians.
- He cares for all people as a loving Father.

Galatians 4:4–6 But when the fullness of time had come, God sent forth His Son, born of woman, born under the law, to redeem those who were under the law, so that we might receive adoption as sons. And because you are sons, God has sent the Spirit of His Son into our hearts, crying, "Abba! Father!"

How did God create everything?

- God spoke, and all things came to be.
- God formed and filled all of creation in six days.

Genesis 1:1, 3, 31 In the beginning, God created the heavens and the earth. . . . And God said, "Let there be light," and there was light. . . . And God saw everything that He had made, and behold, it was very good. And there was evening and there was morning, the sixth day.

How are humans different from all other creatures?

God created man and woman in His image, to live in a special relationship with Him. God breathed life into Adam. Humans are able to reason and have a soul that will never die. God gave humans the job of taking care of His creation.

Genesis 1:26–27 Then God said, "Let Us make man in Our image, after Our likeness. And let them have dominion over the fish of the sea and over the birds of the heavens and over the livestock and over all the earth and over every creeping thing that creeps on the earth." So God created man in His own image, in the image of God He created him; male and female He created them.

What do we know about angels?

God created angels to be His messengers and to serve Him. Angels protect God's people. The devil was an angel who rebelled against God. The devil and other fallen angels now try to destroy God's good creation and lead us away from God. Angels are different from humans. We will not turn into angels when we die.

Psalm 91:11 For He will command His angels concerning you to guard you in all your ways.

A Bible Illustration

God created humans in a special way and gave them a special job. Read about it in Genesis 2:7–25.

What was special about the way that God created Adam and Eve?

What special jobs did God give to Adam and Eve?

Faith Connections

God is good. Have you heard this sentence before? It's true. And because God is good, everything He does is good too. The sun? Good. The stars? Good. The land and water? Good and good. The animals? Yes, good. What about people? Yes. However, when God looked at Adam, He said that it was not good for man to be alone. After God made Eve, He called His work very good. When we look at our world today, we know that many things are not good. That's because sin entered the world, and we live in a broken place. That's why God the Father sent His Son, Jesus, to die and rise. Because Jesus paid for all the sin in the world, we can believe in Jesus and be forgiven. When God the Father looks at you now, a forgiven child, He calls you good. Someday, Jesus will come back. He promises to make a new heaven and a new earth, where nothing will be broken. How good that will be!

 ## Think and Share

Why do we call God "Father"?

How did all things come into being?

Why are humans special?

 ## Sing

Now Thank We All Our God (*LSB* 895:1; *OAR* 336:1)
> Now thank we all our God With hearts and hands and voices,
> Who wondrous things has done, In whom His world rejoices;
> Who from our mothers' arms Has blest us on our way
> With countless gifts of love And still is ours today.

 ## Bible Memory Verse

For by [God] all things were created, in heaven and on earth, visible and invisible. (Colossians 1:16)

 ## Pray

Dear Father God, Creator of all things, I praise You for all the wonderful things You have made. Thank You especially for creating me to be Your own child. Help me care for the beautiful creation You have made. Amen.

I believe in God, the Father Almighty, Maker of heaven and earth.

What does this mean?

He also gives me clothing and shoes, food and drink, house and home, wife and children, land, animals, and all I have. He richly and daily provides me with all that I need to support this body and life. He defends me against all danger and guards and protects me from all evil.

Understanding the First Article (Part 2): God's Care

- God continues to be active in the world He created.
- God takes care of His creation and cares for all His creatures.
- God gives people everything they need to live.
- God protects us from danger and evil.

> **THE MAIN IDEA**
> I believe that God takes care of me and His creation and gives me all that I need for this life. He protects me from danger and evil.

Learning about the First Article (Part 2): God's Care

Does God continue to take care of the world He created?

Yes. God is with us, looking after His creation and creating new life in it.

Job 12:10 In His hand is the life of every living thing and the breath of all mankind.

How does God care for His creation and especially for His human creation?

God gives rain and sun to the earth. He gives food for the animals. God gives people food, drink, clothing, and shelter. He blesses people with family, friends, work, health, and joy. He protects us from danger and evil.

Psalm 104:14–15 You cause the grass to grow for the livestock and plants for man to cultivate, that he may bring forth food from the earth and wine to gladden the heart of man, oil to make his face shine and bread to strengthen man's heart.

Psalm 121:2, 7   My help comes from the LORD, who made heaven and earth. . . . The LORD will keep you from all evil; He will keep your life.

If God cares for His creation, why is there pain and suffering in the world?

God created a perfect world, but Adam and Eve brought evil into the world when they disobeyed God. Now the whole world is damaged by sin and brokenness. Sin causes suffering and death.

Romans 5:12   Therefore, just as sin came into the world through one man, and death through sin, and so death spread to all men because all sinned.

What is God doing about all the suffering and death in the world?

God sent Jesus to take our suffering and the punishment for our sins onto Himself when He died on the cross. By His death and resurrection, Jesus defeated sin and death and gives us eternal life. God works all things, even bad things, for our good. He works through His people to show mercy and love to others.

Romans 5:8   God shows His love for us in that while we were still sinners, Christ died for us.

Romans 8:28   And we know that for those who love God all things work together for good, for those who are called according to His purpose.

A Bible Illustration

Read how the psalmist talks about the way God cares for His creation in Psalm 104:10–30.

How does the psalmist describe God's care for the earth?

How does the psalmist describe God's care for His creatures?

Faith Connections

Imagine that your favorite toy or device breaks. Even if you can fix it, it will never be quite right. That's a little like our world. God made a beautiful, perfect world. When Adam and Eve sinned, the world became broken and damaged with sin and evil. There is still a lot of beauty and goodness in the world, but things aren't quite right. Still, God continues to give us everything we need: food, clothing, health, and more. Jesus came to save us from sin and death, and He promises to come back again. When that happens, everything will be perfect again! As we wait, we can help show God's love in a broken world so that more people can know and be ready for Jesus when He returns.

 ## Think and Share

Name some of the ways that God takes care of His creation.

What are some ways that God takes care of you?

How can you thank God for all His loving care? Can you say a prayer, sing a song of praise, or tell others about Him?

 ## Sing

I Believe (*OAR* 347:1)
> I believe my heav'nly Father, God Almighty throned above,
> Cares for me and all His creatures In His ever-gracious love.
> See what precious gifts He sends us! This is how I know He cares:
> He sent Jesus here to save us From the sin that would enslave us.
> Holy Father, hear our prayers!

 ## Bible Memory Verse

> The eyes of all look to You, and You give them their food in due season.
> (Psalm 145:15)

 ## Pray

Dear God, thank You for giving me all that I need to live and for protecting me from danger and evil. Help me to look to You for everything and to give You thanks and praise for all Your good gifts. In Jesus' name I pray. Amen.

I believe in God, the Father Almighty, Maker of heaven and earth.

What does this mean?

All this He does only out of fatherly, divine goodness and mercy, without any merit or worthiness in me. For all this it is my duty to thank and praise, serve and obey Him. This is most certainly true.

Understanding the First Article (Part 3): God's Grace

- God made and cares for all creation out of fatherly goodness, mercy, and love.
- We do not deserve all that God has made and done for us.
- We should thank and praise, serve and obey God because of all that He has done for us.

> **THE MAIN IDEA**
> I believe that every good thing in my life is an undeserved gift from God.

Learning about the First Article (Part 3): God's Grace

What does it mean that God made and cares for all creation "out of fatherly, divine goodness and mercy"?

God did not have to create the world. He did it out of love. God cares for us as our heavenly Father, even though we are sinful.

Psalm 136:1, 5, 24–25 Give thanks to the LORD, for He is good, for His steadfast love endures forever. . . . To Him who by understanding made the heavens, for His steadfast love endures forever; . . . and rescued us from our foes, for His steadfast love endures forever; He who gives food to all flesh, for His steadfast love endures forever.

Is there anything we can do to deserve God's love and care for us?

No. There is nothing we can do to deserve what God has done for us. God gives us all good things, including salvation, because He loves us and has mercy on us.

Psalm 103:13 As a father shows compassion to his children, so the LORD shows compassion to those who fear Him.

How do we show thankfulness to God for all He has done for us?

We can tell God through prayers and songs how thankful we are for what He has done. We also show thankfulness by obeying His Commandments and serving Him and other people.

Psalm 95:1–3 Oh come, let us sing to the LORD; let us make a joyful noise to the rock of our salvation! Let us come into His presence with thanksgiving; let us make a joyful noise to Him with songs of praise! For the LORD is a great God, and a great King above all gods.

A Bible Illustration

Jesus showed how much He cares for people's daily needs when He provided food to eat for over five thousand people. Read about it in Matthew 14:13–21.

What needs did the people have?

How did Jesus show that He cared about the crowds of people?

Faith Connections

Imagine that you just received the best gift ever! It was free, and it is amazing. Even better, there are lots more of the same gift to go around! What would you do? You would probably want to tell all your friends. Why? First, you'd be very excited. Second, you would want them to have the same cool gift too. Guess what. You *do* have the very best gift! You have grace and forgiveness in Jesus Christ. It's free for you, and it's free for everyone. Not only that, but you also have lots of other gifts too: food, clothing, and more. So, what are you waiting for? Go tell others about this amazing gift of God's grace! And if you have plenty of those other gifts (clothing, food, and so on), you can share those too. That way, others can see Jesus' love and blessings through you. What a great gift that is!

 ## Think and Share

Make a top-ten list of the things you are thankful for. Why does God give us many blessings?

Do we have the right to demand that God give us things? Why or why not?

What is one way you can thank God for all He has done for you?

 ## Sing

O God, My Faithful God (*LSB* 696:1)
> O God, my faithful God, True fountain ever flowing,
> Without whom nothing is, All perfect gifts bestowing:
> Give me a healthy frame, And may I have within
> A conscience free from blame, A soul unstained by sin.

 ## Bible Memory Verse

Every good gift and every perfect gift is from above, coming down from the Father of lights. (James 1:17)

 ## Pray

Dear God, thank You for all Your good gifts to me! I know that I do not deserve them. Help me remember to thank and praise You every day. Help me show my thankfulness by obeying You and serving others. In Jesus' name I pray. Amen.

THE SECOND ARTICLE (PART 1): JESUS—TRUE GOD AND TRUE MAN

And [I believe] in Jesus Christ, His only Son, our Lord, who was conceived by the Holy Spirit, born of the Virgin Mary, suffered under Pontius Pilate, was crucified, died and was buried. He descended into hell. The third day He rose again from the dead. He ascended into heaven and sits at the right hand of God, the Father Almighty. From thence He will come to judge the living and the dead.

What does this mean?
I believe that Jesus Christ, true God, begotten of the Father from eternity, and also true man, born of the Virgin Mary, is my Lord.

Understanding the Second Article (Part 1): Jesus—True God and True Man

- Jesus is true God. He existed before the creation of the world, and He created all things together with the Father and the Spirit.
- Jesus is true man. He is human, just as we are human, but He has no sin.
- Jesus came down from heaven, became a human baby, and was born of the Virgin Mary.

Learning about the Second Article (Part 1): Jesus—True God and True Man

What does it mean that Jesus is my Lord?

Jesus rules over all things as our Creator and the Savior of all mankind. Jesus is the Lord God Himself, in human flesh.

Colossians 1:16, 19–20 For by [Jesus] all things were created, in heaven and on earth, visible and invisible, whether thrones or dominions or rulers or authorities—all things were created through Him and for Him. . . . For in Him all the fullness of God was pleased to dwell, and through Him to reconcile to Himself all things, whether on earth or in heaven, making peace by the blood of His cross.

> **THE MAIN IDEA**
> I believe that Jesus Christ, the Son of God, is true God and true man.

Why do we confess that Jesus is true God?

- Jesus existed before the creation of the world and created all things together with the Father and the Spirit.
- The Bible calls Jesus God, and Jesus did things that only God can do.

John 1:1–2 In the beginning was the Word, and the Word was with God, and the Word was God. He was in the beginning with God.

Why do we confess that Jesus is true man?

- Jesus, the Son of God, became a human being with a human body and soul.
- The Bible calls Him man, and Jesus did human things, such as eat and sleep.

Matthew 1:22–23 All this took place to fulfill what the Lord had spoken by the prophet: "Behold, the virgin shall conceive and bear a son, and they shall call His name Immanuel" (which means, God with us).

Why is it so important that Jesus is both true God and true man?

- Jesus, as true man, kept God's Law perfectly on our behalf. He died to take the punishment for our sins, and He rose from the dead, defeating death.
- As true God, Jesus' life, suffering, and death were enough to pay for the sins of all people. His resurrection was enough to rescue all people from death.

Galatians 4:4–5 But when the fullness of time had come, God sent forth His Son, born of woman, born under the law, to redeem those who were under the law, so that we might receive adoption as sons.

A Bible Illustration

At first, the disciple Thomas wouldn't believe that Jesus had risen from the dead. Then he saw Jesus with his own eyes. Read about it in John 20:24–29.

Why didn't Thomas believe that Jesus was alive?

Why do you think Thomas called Jesus "my Lord and my God"?

Faith Connections

There is no one like Jesus. He is the only person of the Trinity who is also man. He is the only man who is also God. This is very hard to understand, but it is an amazing truth! Jesus knows what it is like to be sad, hungry, hurt, and happy. He also has the power to conquer the devil and all evil. It's great to know that we have a God who understands how we feel. It's also great to know that our God has the power to save us. We can pray to Jesus, knowing that He knows what it's like to live here on earth. Because Jesus lived, died, and rose again, we will one day live with Him forever.

 ## Think and Share

What is one thing you know about Jesus that shows He is true God?

What is one thing you know about Jesus that shows He is true man?

When did Jesus become a man?

How would you describe Jesus to someone who doesn't know who He is?

 ## Sing

Beautiful Savior (*LSB* 537:1; *OAR* 237:1)
> Beautiful Savior, King of creation,
> Son of God and Son of Man!
> Truly I'd love Thee, Truly I'd serve Thee,
> Light of my soul, my joy, my crown.

 ## Bible Memory Verse

"Behold, the virgin shall conceive and bear a son, and they shall call His name Immanuel" (which means, God with us). (Matthew 1:23)

 ## Pray

Dear God, thank You for sending Your Son, Jesus Christ, to be my Savior. Help me to believe and trust in Him as true God and true man, my God and Lord, Creator and Redeemer. Amen.

And [I believe] in Jesus Christ, His only Son, our Lord, who was conceived by the Holy Spirit, born of the Virgin Mary, suffered under Pontius Pilate, was crucified, died and was buried. He descended into hell. The third day He rose again from the dead. He ascended into heaven and sits at the right hand of God, the Father Almighty. From thence He will come to judge the living and the dead.

What does this mean?

[Jesus] has redeemed me, a lost and condemned person, purchased and won me from all sins, from death, and from the power of the devil; not with gold or silver, but with His holy, precious blood and with His innocent suffering and death.

Understanding the Second Article (Part 2): Jesus—Redeemer

- All people are born sinful and are lost sinners who are separated from God and face the punishment of eternal death.

- Jesus willingly went to the cross to *redeem* (rescue) us from the powers of sin, death, and the devil.

- Jesus obeyed God's Law perfectly in our place and paid the full punishment for our sins on the cross.

- Jesus defeated death by His death on the cross and His resurrection from the grave. Because Jesus lives, we will also live eternally!

> **THE MAIN IDEA**
> I believe that Jesus willingly died on the cross in order to rescue me from sin, death, and the power of the devil.

Learning about the Second Article (Part 2): Jesus—Redeemer

What does it mean that Jesus redeemed us?

Jesus rescued us and took us back from evil powers that kept us away from God.

Colossians 1:13–14 He has delivered us from the domain of darkness and transferred us to the kingdom of His beloved Son, in whom we have redemption, the forgiveness of sins.

Why did we need to be redeemed?

The devil tempted Adam and Eve to disobey God, and sin came into the world. Every person is born sinful and continues to disobey God. The devil continues to tempt us to sin and turn away from God. The punishment for sin is eternal death.

Romans 5:12   Therefore, just as sin came into the world through one man, and death through sin, and so death spread to all men because all sinned.

Why did God send Jesus to redeem us?

God sent His Son to save us and bring us back to Him because He loves us.

John 3:16   For God so loved the world, that He gave His only Son, that whoever believes in Him should not perish but have eternal life.

How did Jesus rescue me from sin, death, and the devil?

When Jesus died on the cross, He paid the full punishment for my sin. Jesus obeyed God's will perfectly in my place, defeating the power of the devil over me. Jesus destroyed the power of death over me by His own death and resurrection.

1 Peter 1:18–19   You were ransomed from the futile ways inherited from your forefathers, not with perishable things such as silver or gold, but with the precious blood of Christ, like that of a lamb without blemish or spot.

What does the Bible teach about Jesus' resurrection?

The Bible teaches that Jesus rose from the dead on the third day. Jesus' resurrection proves that He is the Son of God and that God the Father has accepted Jesus' sacrifice. Everyone who believes in Jesus will have eternal life.

John 14:19   Because I live, you also will live.

A Bible Illustration

Jesus willingly died on the cross to pay for all our sins. Read about it in Luke 23:32–56.

What do these Bible verses tell you about Jesus?

What do these verses tell you about how Jesus feels about you?

Faith Connections

Has anyone ever taken the blame for something you did wrong? Jesus takes the blame for everything all people have done wrong. Adam failed to be the man he was created to be. As a son, he disobeyed his Father. Jesus is the man that Adam could not be. As the Son, Jesus obeyed His Father. Jesus took Adam's place. He takes our place too. Jesus lived the life we couldn't live. Jesus died the death we were supposed to die. And because He rose again, guess what! We'll rise too! When Jesus took our place, He gave us His place: His place as holy and beloved and everlasting. How amazing! Thanks to Jesus, we get to live with Him forever.

 ## Think and Share

Why do we (and all people) need a Savior?

What are some of the evils in this world that try to take us away from God?

What did Jesus do to save you?

How does Jesus' death and resurrection give you hope and joy?

 ## Sing

Chief of Sinners Though I Be (*LSB* 611:1)
> Chief of sinners though I be, Jesus shed His blood for me.
> Died that I might live on high, Lives that I might never die.
> As the branch is to the vine, I am His, and He is mine.

 ## Bible Memory Verse

Christ died for our sins. (1 Corinthians 15:3)

 ## Pray

Dear Jesus, thank You for the great love that You have for me and all people. Thank You for willingly going to the cross to pay for my sins and the sins of the whole world. Help me to live a life that honors You. In Your name I pray. Amen.

And [I believe] in Jesus Christ, His only Son, our Lord, who was conceived by the Holy Spirit, born of the Virgin Mary, suffered under Pontius Pilate, was crucified, died and was buried. He descended into hell. The third day He rose again from the dead. He ascended into heaven and sits at the right hand of God, the Father Almighty. From thence He will come to judge the living and the dead.

What does this mean?

That I may be His own and live under Him in His kingdom and serve Him in everlasting righteousness, innocence, and blessedness, just as He is risen from the dead, lives and reigns to all eternity. This is most certainly true.

Understanding the Second Article (Part 3): Jesus—Prophet, Priest, and King

- Jesus redeemed me so that I can live with Him and for Him, now and forever.
- I belong to Jesus Christ. He is mine, and I am His. He cares for me.
- Jesus is my Prophet, Priest, and King.

> **THE MAIN IDEA**
> I believe that Jesus redeemed me so that I may live under His care and serve Him and others.

Learning about the Second Article (Part 3): Jesus—Prophet, Priest, and King

Why did Jesus free me from sin, death, and the devil?

Jesus did this to be my Lord, so that I can live with Him and for Him in peace and joy, both now and forever.

2 Corinthians 5:15 He died for all, that those who live might no longer live for themselves but for Him who for their sake died and was raised.

What does it mean that I belong to Jesus Christ and live under Him in His kingdom?

Jesus is mine, and I am His child. Jesus is my loving King who rules over me to defend and protect me. Jesus sends the Holy Spirit to be with me and teach me.

Galatians 2:20 I have been crucified with Christ. It is no longer I who live, but Christ who lives in me. And the life I now live in the flesh I live by faith in the Son of God, who loved me and gave Himself for me.

How does Jesus give my life purpose?

I serve Jesus now as I live as His child here on this earth. Because Jesus rose from the dead, I know that I will one day live with Him and serve Him perfectly in heaven.

Philippians 1:6 He who began a good work in you will bring it to completion at the day of Jesus Christ.

What does it mean that Jesus is our Prophet, Priest, and King?

- As our Prophet, Jesus proclaims God's Word to us.
- As our Priest, Jesus offered Himself as the sacrifice for our sin, and He speaks to the Father on our behalf.
- As our King, Jesus rules over all of creation and cares for His Church.

Hebrews 1:1–2 Long ago, at many times and in many ways, God spoke to our fathers by the prophets, but in these last days He has spoken to us by His Son.

Hebrews 7:26–27 For it was indeed fitting that we should have such a high priest, holy, innocent, unstained, separated from sinners, and exalted above the heavens. He has no need, like those high priests, to offer sacrifices daily, first for His own sins and then for those of the people, since He did this once for all when He offered up Himself.

A Bible Illustration

When Jesus rose from the dead, it changed the disciples' lives. Read about it in Luke 24:36–53.

How did the disciples first react when they saw Jesus alive?

After Jesus opened their eyes to the truth, what did the disciples do?

Faith Connections

In the Old Testament, three types of leaders were prophets, priests, and kings. Prophets shared the Word of God with others. Priests prayed and offered sacrifices on behalf of the people. Kings ruled over the people and cared for them on God's behalf. How does Jesus do all these things? Jesus gives the Word of God because He *is* the Word of God. Jesus is the ultimate priestly sacrifice, paying for all our sins and earning our forgiveness. Jesus is the King of kings.

God works through us too. We share God's Word with others. He uses us as a priesthood of believers—praying for others even when they can't pray for themselves. We go out to the world, representing the King of kings to all.

 ## Think and Share

What does it mean to you that you belong to Jesus?

How can you live as God's child on this earth?

Talk about why we call Jesus our Prophet, Priest, and King.

 ## Sing

Let Us Ever Walk with Jesus (*LSB* 685:4)

> Let us also live with Jesus. He has risen from the dead
> That to life we may awaken. Jesus, You are now our head.
> We are Your own living members; Where You live, there we shall be
> In Your presence constantly, Living there with You forever.
> Jesus, let me faithful be, Life eternal grant to me.

 ## Bible Memory Verse

But you are a chosen race, a royal priesthood, a holy nation, a people for His own possession, that you may proclaim the excellencies of Him who called you out of darkness into His marvelous light. (1 Peter 2:9)

 ## Pray

Dear Jesus, You are my Savior and my King. Thank You for making me Yours. Help me to live for You in all that I say and do. Give me faith to trust in Your promise that one day, I will live in Your heavenly kingdom with You forever. Amen.

THE THIRD ARTICLE (PART 1): WORK OF THE HOLY SPIRIT

I believe in the Holy Spirit, the holy Christian church, the communion of saints, the forgiveness of sins, the resurrection of the body, and the life everlasting. Amen.

What does this mean?

I believe that I cannot by my own reason or strength believe in Jesus Christ, my Lord, or come to Him; but the Holy Spirit has called me by the Gospel, enlightened me with His gifts, sanctified and kept me in the true faith.

Understanding the Third Article (Part 1): Work of the Holy Spirit

- The Holy Spirit is true God with the Father and the Son.

- Without the Holy Spirit's work, we cannot understand anything about Jesus and we cannot do anything to believe in Him.

- The Holy Spirit creates saving faith in us, enabling us to believe in Jesus as our Savior.

- The Holy Spirit keeps us in the faith and helps us lead a life that is pleasing to God.

> **THE MAIN IDEA**
> I believe that the Holy Spirit brings me to faith in Jesus Christ through the Gospel.

Learning about the Third Article (Part 1): Work of the Holy Spirit

Who is the Holy Spirit?

The Holy Spirit is God. He is one of the three persons of the Trinity, along with the Father and the Son.

Matthew 28:19 Go therefore and make disciples of all nations, baptizing them in the name of the Father and of the Son and of the Holy Spirit.

Why can't I come to faith in Jesus "by my own reason or strength"?

Without the Holy Spirit, we have no understanding of Jesus and cannot trust in Him. Without the Holy Spirit, I do not want to believe in Jesus as my Savior.

1 Corinthians 2:14   The natural person does not accept the things of the Spirit of God, for they are folly to him, and he is not able to understand them because they are spiritually discerned.

1 Corinthians 12:3   Therefore I want you to understand that no one speaking in the Spirit of God ever says "Jesus is accursed!" And no one can say "Jesus is Lord" except in the Holy Spirit.

How does the Holy Spirit bring people to faith in Jesus?

The Holy Spirit creates faith in people through the Gospel (the Good News about Jesus, our Savior) so they believe that Jesus loves them and died for their sins.

John 3:5–6   Jesus answered, "Truly, truly, I say to you, unless one is born of water and the Spirit, he cannot enter the kingdom of God. That which is born of the flesh is flesh, and that which is born of the Spirit is spirit."

Romans 1:16   For I am not ashamed of the gospel, for it is the power of God for salvation to everyone who believes.

What does it mean to be sanctified by the Spirit?

To be *sanctified* means "to be made holy." The Spirit makes us holy by bringing us to Jesus, by strengthening our faith, and by helping us to live lives that are pleasing to God.

Galatians 5:22–23   But the fruit of the Spirit is love, joy, peace, patience, kindness, goodness, faithfulness, gentleness, self-control; against such things there is no law.

A Bible Illustration

The Holy Spirit worked in Lydia's heart as she heard Paul preach the Word of God. Read about it in Acts 16:13–15.

How did Lydia become a believer?

What did Lydia do after she was baptized?

Faith Connections

We can do nothing. We can do all things. Both of these sentences are true. But how? They seem to be opposites.

We can do nothing: There is nothing that we can do to save ourselves. There is nothing we can do to make God love us more—or even love us less. There is nothing we can do to have faith. When it comes to our salvation, there is nothing we can do. God does it all. That is *great* news!

So now that we are free and saved and secure in the hand of God, we can do all kinds of things with His help. God plans good works for us to do and gives us what we need to do them. God gives us strength to love and forgive others. We don't have to be afraid that we're doing too little or too much or not perfectly. God the Father takes the things we do and makes them good through forgiveness in Jesus and the power of the Holy Spirit.

 ## Think and Share

When is it difficult to show love to someone? Ask for God's help. He will give you the strength to help others, even when it's hard to do!

 ## Sing

O Holy Spirit, Enter In (*LSB* 913:1)
> O Holy Spirit, enter in, And in our hearts Your work begin,
> Your dwelling place now make us. Sun of the soul, O Light divine,
> Around and in us brightly shine, To joy and gladness wake us
> That we may be Truly living, To You giving Prayer unceasing
> And in love be still increasing.

 ## Bible Memory Verse

No one can say "Jesus is Lord" except in the Holy Spirit. (1 Corinthians 12:3)

 ## Pray

O Holy Spirit, thank You for leading me to faith in Jesus as my Savior. Strengthen my faith so that I live a God-pleasing life. Keep me in the true faith until life everlasting. Amen.

THE THIRD ARTICLE (PART 2): THE HOLY CHRISTIAN CHURCH

I believe in the Holy Spirit, the holy Christian church, the communion of saints, the forgiveness of sins, the resurrection of the body, and the life everlasting. Amen.

What does this mean?
In the same way He calls, gathers, enlightens, and sanctifies the whole Christian church on earth, and keeps it with Jesus Christ in the one true faith. In this Christian church He daily and richly forgives all my sins and the sins of all believers.

Understanding the Third Article (Part 2): The Holy Christian Church

- The Holy Spirit brings me to faith in Jesus and makes me a member of the Church.
- The Church is made up of believers in Jesus throughout the world.
- The Church is also called the Body of Christ. Jesus is the Head of the Church.
- God forgives our sins for Jesus' sake. We receive forgiveness by believing the promise of the Gospel, the Good News about Jesus, our Savior.

> **THE MAIN IDEA**
> I believe that the Holy Spirit brings all believers together into a community we call the Church.

Learning about the Third Article (Part 2): The Holy Christian Church

What is the Church?

The Church is made up of all people throughout the world whom the Holy Spirit has brought to faith in Christ. The Church is also called the Body of Christ. We cannot see the Church. Only God can see if someone believes.

1 Corinthians 12:12–13 For just as the body is one and has many members, and all the members of the body, though many, are one body, so it is with Christ. For in one Spirit we were all baptized into one body.

Ephesians 2:19–20   So then you are no longer strangers and aliens, but you are fellow citizens with the saints and members of the household of God, built on the foundation of the apostles and prophets, Christ Jesus Himself being the cornerstone.

What is the communion of saints?

Saints are "holy ones," people who have been forgiven of their sins. A *communion* is a group of people who share the same faith.

1 Corinthians 1:2   To the church of God that is in Corinth, to those sanctified in Christ Jesus, called to be saints together with all those who in every place call upon the name of our Lord Jesus Christ, both their Lord and ours . . .

What is the mission (job) of the Church on earth?

The Church's mission is to proclaim the forgiveness of sins for Jesus' sake by proclaiming God's Word, offering the Sacraments, and living as God's people.

Matthew 28:19   Go therefore and make disciples of all nations, baptizing them in the name of the Father and of the Son and of the Holy Spirit.

Acts 2:42   And they devoted themselves to the apostles' teaching and the fellowship, to the breaking of bread and the prayers.

What is the forgiveness of sins?

God, in love and mercy, promises not to give us the punishment for our sins that we deserve. He forgives us because of Christ's work on the cross.

Ephesians 1:7   In [Jesus] we have redemption through His blood, the forgiveness of our trespasses, according to the riches of His grace.

A Bible Illustration

After Pentecost, believers in Jesus gathered together to pray and study God's Word. Read about it in Acts 2:42–47.

What did the believers in Jesus do together?

How was the Holy Spirit working in the hearts and lives of the believers?

Faith Connections

Did you realize you have billions of brothers and sisters? How? God the Father calls us His children through His Word and in Baptism. If we all have the same heavenly Father, that means we have lots of brothers and sisters all over the world.

Ready to think about something even more amazing? God calls us a Body. That's one way God describes the Church. Jesus is the Head of the Body. We are all parts of the Body. We serve as hands that help, feet that go, arms that hug, and mouths that speak. The Holy Spirit lives in us and joins us together. Imagine one big body of people, led by Jesus, and united with one Spirit—the very Spirit of God.

In Jesus, we are all connected in one family. We are all connected in one Body. We are all connected to one another because we believe in Jesus Christ. How does that make you feel, knowing that you are connected with so many others?

 ## Think and Share

Who is part of the Church, the Body of Christ?

What is one important job of the Church?

 ## Sing

The Church's One Foundation (*LSB* 644:1)
> The Church's one foundation Is Jesus Christ, her Lord;
> She is His new creation By water and the Word.
> From heav'n He came and sought her To be His holy bride;
> With His own blood He bought her, And for her life He died.

 ## Bible Memory Verse

> Now you are the body of Christ and individually members of it.
> (1 Corinthians 12:27)

 ## Pray

Heavenly Father, thank You for gathering all believers together and making us into Your Church. Thank You for the forgiveness of sins in Jesus. Keep me and all believers united in the true faith. Help us to proclaim Your Good News to the world. In Jesus' name I pray. Amen.

THE THIRD ARTICLE (PART 3): RESURRECTION AND LIFE EVERLASTING

I believe in the Holy Spirit, the holy Christian church, the communion of saints, the forgiveness of sins, the resurrection of the body, and the life everlasting. Amen.

What does this mean?

On the Last Day He will raise me and all the dead, and give eternal life to me and all believers in Christ. This is most certainly true.

Understanding the Third Article (Part 3): Resurrection and Life Everlasting

- Jesus will come back to earth to judge the living and the dead. He will take all believers to be with Him in heaven forever, but unbelievers will go to eternal death.

> **THE MAIN IDEA**
> I believe that Jesus will one day return to raise all those who have died and give eternal life to all believers.

- Jesus will change our bodies to be perfect and new. The old heaven and earth will pass away, and He will create a new heaven and a new earth.

- Satan will be defeated forever and sent away to eternal punishment.

- Believers will see God face-to-face and will live forever with Him in perfect peace and happiness.

Learning about the Third Article (Part 3): Resurrection and Life Everlasting

What will happen on the Last Day when Jesus returns?

Jesus will return in glory, all the dead will be raised, and Christ will judge all people. Believers will be given eternal life, but unbelievers will go to eternal death.

John 5:24, 28–29 Truly, truly, I say to you, whoever hears My word and believes Him who sent Me has eternal life. . . . Do not marvel at this, for an hour is coming when all who are in the tombs will hear His voice and come out, those who have done good to the resurrection of life, and those who have done evil to the resurrection of judgment.

What else will happen on the Last Day?

Jesus will change our bodies to be perfect and new; Satan will be defeated forever and sent away to eternal punishment; the heavens and earth will be made new again; we will see God face-to-face; and God will dwell with us forever.

Philippians 3:21 [He] will transform our lowly body to be like His glorious body, by the power that enables Him even to subject all things to Himself.

Revelation 21:1, 3 Then I saw a new heaven and a new earth, for the first heaven and the first earth had passed away, and the sea was no more. . . . And I heard a loud voice from the throne saying, "Behold, the dwelling place of God is with man. He will dwell with them, and they will be His people, and God Himself will be with them as their God."

What will happen to me when I am raised from the dead on the Last Day?

I will enjoy being with Jesus in His new creation, in body and soul, forever.

1 Corinthians 15:51–52 Behold! I tell you a mystery. We shall not all sleep, but we shall all be changed, in a moment, in the twinkling of an eye, at the last trumpet. For the trumpet will sound, and the dead will be raised imperishable, and we shall be changed.

Do we know when Jesus will return? What should we do as we wait for His return?

No. No one knows when the Last Day will come. As we wait, we should be watchful, pray that the Holy Spirit would keep us in the true faith, and share the Gospel with as many people as possible.

Matthew 24:44 Therefore you also must be ready, for the Son of Man is coming at an hour you do not expect.

A Bible Illustration

Jesus talked about a day when He will return. Read about it in John 5:24–29.

Who will have eternal life?

Why can we look forward to Jesus' return?

Faith Connections

Some people say that it's good to act like every day is your last. The idea is that you would be more thankful for the day and would use it wisely, as if every moment mattered.

A pastor once told his congregation, "It may be an even better idea to live like Jesus was coming back today." Why would that be better? Well, for one thing, it's true. Jesus could come at any moment, and it will be a big surprise for everyone when He comes back. Another reason is that it takes the focus from yourself and makes you think of other people. You know that you will live with Jesus. But if Jesus is coming back, that impacts everyone.

Ask yourself, Who else needs to know about Jesus to be ready for His return? Suddenly, you're thinking about other people too. When Jesus comes back, people will rise from the dead. Evil will go away forever. Everything will be made new. What great news! What can you do to share this news today?

Think and Share

Believers in Jesus look forward to Jesus' return with joy, not fear. Why?

How do you imagine Jesus' return? Draw a picture.

Who will you share the Good News of Jesus with this week? Make a plan, then do it!

Sing

The King Shall Come When Morning Dawns (*LSB* 348:4)
> Oh, brighter than that glorious morn Shall dawn upon our race
> The day when Christ in splendor comes And we shall see His face.

Bible Memory Verse

For I know that my Redeemer lives, and at the last He will stand upon the earth. (Job 19:25)

Pray

Dear Jesus, thank You for Your great love for me and all people! Send Your Spirit to keep me strong in my faith and to help me share the Good News of Your love and forgiveness with others. Amen.

Introduction to the Lord's Prayer

The Lord's Prayer is the prayer that Jesus gave to His disciples and to all believers so that we know how to pray and what we are to pray for.

- The Lord's Prayer teaches us to look to God for all that we need. In the first three *petitions* (requests), we pray for things about God. In the last four petitions, we pray for our physical and spiritual needs.

- Prayer is speaking to God in words and thoughts.

- God invites us to come to Him in prayer. He promises to hear our prayers and even gives us words that we can say.

- God always answers our prayers. God answers in His own time and in His own way, for our good.

Our Father who art in heaven.

What does this mean?
With these words God tenderly invites us to believe that He is our true Father and that we are His true children, so that with all boldness and confidence we may ask Him as dear children ask their dear father.

Understanding the Introduction

- Jesus invites us to call upon God as our heavenly Father.

- We are to pray only to the one true God and not to anyone or anything else.

- We call on our heavenly Father in prayer, and we pray in the name of Jesus.

- We may also pray to Jesus and the Holy Spirit, because they are one with the Father.

> **THE MAIN IDEA**
> God invites us to talk to Him in prayer, calling on Him as our loving heavenly Father.

Learning about the Introduction

How does Jesus invite us to pray?

- Jesus invites us to call on God as "our Father."
- We pray with confidence, knowing that God our Father wants to help us.
- We pray with and for all Christians, who are our brothers and sisters in Christ.

Matthew 6:9 Pray then like this: "Our Father in heaven, hallowed be Your name."

Hebrews 4:16 Let us then with confidence draw near to the throne of grace, that we may receive mercy and find grace to help in time of need.

Why are we able to call God our Father?
We have been adopted as God's children through faith in Jesus Christ.

1 John 3:1 See what kind of love the Father has given to us, that we should be called children of God; and so we are.

Why do we call Him our Father who is "in heaven"?

We are not calling on an earthly father. He is our heavenly Father, who is God and Lord over all creation.

Acts 17:24   The God who made the world and everything in it, being Lord of heaven and earth, does not live in temples made by man.

To whom are we to pray?

We are to pray only to the one true God, the Father, Son, and Holy Spirit. We are not to pray to anything or anyone else.

Matthew 4:9–10   And [the devil] said to Him, "All these I will give You, if You will fall down and worship me." Then Jesus said to him, "Be gone, Satan! For it is written, 'You shall worship the Lord your God and Him only shall you serve.'"

How does the New Testament teach us to pray?

The New Testament teaches us to pray to the Father, and to pray in Jesus' name. We may pray to Jesus and the Holy Spirit, because they are one God with the Father.

John 16:23   Truly, truly, I say to you, whatever you ask of the Father in My name, He will give it to you.

A Bible Illustration

Jesus told a parable about a loving father. Read about it in Luke 15:11–32.

What did the father do when he saw his son returning home?

What does this parable tell us about the love of God our Father?

Faith Connections

Who do you go to when you need help? How wonderful it is to be able to call out to your dad or mom or caregiver when you have troubles or when you need something.

Jesus reminds us in the Lord's Prayer that there is someone who cares even more for you than your dad, mom, or caregiver. It is your Father in heaven. He is the one who created you and loves you, the one who knows everything about you and saved you through Jesus, the one who has the power to help you, no matter what you need. Our parents and caregivers aren't perfect; they make mistakes. But our heavenly Father always keeps His promises and will love you no matter what.

Call on your dear heavenly Father. He promises to hear you and to help you.

Think and Share

God calls you His child. How does that make you feel?

Have you memorized the Lord's Prayer? If not, begin with the Introduction today. Add other petitions as you study them.

Sing

What a Friend We Have in Jesus (*LSB* 770:1; *OAR* 287:1)

> What a friend we have in Jesus, All our sins and griefs to bear!
> What a privilege to carry Ev'rything to God in prayer!
> Oh, what peace we often forfeit; Oh, what needless pain we bear—
> All because we do not carry Ev'rything to God in prayer!

Bible Memory Verse

> Truly, truly, I say to you, whatever you ask of the Father in My name, He will give it to you. (John 16:23)

Pray

Dear Father in heaven, thank You for inviting me to come and talk to You in prayer about everything I need. I know that You promise to hear all my prayers, that You have the power to help, and that You want to help me. Thank You for calling me Your child! In Jesus' name I pray. Amen.

FIRST PETITION

Hallowed be Thy name.

What does this mean?
God's name is certainly holy in itself, but we pray in this petition that it may be kept holy among us also.

How is God's name kept holy?
God's name is kept holy when the Word of God is taught in its truth and purity, and we, as the children of God, also lead holy lives according to it. Help us to do this, dear Father in heaven! But anyone who teaches or lives contrary to God's Word profanes the name of God among us. Protect us from this, heavenly Father!

Understanding the First Petition

- We *hallow* God's name by keeping His name holy.
- We keep God's name holy by honoring and respecting His Word both with the words we say and also with the lives we live.
- We dishonor God's name when we teach things and live lives that are against God's Word.
- We should gently and lovingly correct anyone who dishonors God and His name.

> **THE MAIN IDEA**
> To hallow God's name is to keep His name holy. We pray that God would help us keep His name holy by speaking truthfully about His Word and living according to His Word.

Learning about the First Petition

What is the connection between this petition and the Second Commandment?

Both talk about the name of God and how we use it. We are not to misuse God's name, or treat it disrespectfully, but we are to use it in a good way, showing honor and respect to Him.

Exodus 20:7 You shall not take the name of the LORD your God in vain, for the LORD will not hold him guiltless who takes His name in vain.

What do we mean by "God's name"?

God cannot be separated from His name. God's name includes who He is, what He does, and how He lives among us.

Psalm 9:1–2   I will give thanks to the Lord with my whole heart; I will recount all of Your wonderful deeds. I will be glad and exult in You; I will sing praise to Your name, O Most High.

What are we asking of God when we pray to keep God's name holy?

We ask God to help us speak truthfully about His Word and to help us live lives that follow the teachings of God's Word.

Matthew 5:16   In the same way, let your light shine before others, so that they may see your good works and give glory to your Father who is in heaven.

How is God's name profaned (dishonored and disrespected)?

God's name is profaned when someone presents a false teaching as God's Word or when someone lives in a way that is against God's will and Word.

Jeremiah 23:31   Behold, I am against the prophets, declares the Lord, who use their tongues and declare, "declares the Lord."

How should we talk with those who dishonor God's name?

We should gently correct those who misuse God's name by what they say, how they live, or what they teach.

Galatians 6:1   Brothers, if anyone is caught in any transgression, you who are spiritual should restore him in a spirit of gentleness. Keep watch on yourself, lest you too be tempted.

A Bible Illustration

The psalmist writes that all of creation is to praise God's name. Read Psalm 148.

Why should the name of the Lord be praised? What has He done for His creation and His people?

How can you praise the name of the Lord today?

Faith Connections

Think about the ways that people can say your name. How does your grandparent say your name? How does your best friend say your name when you see each other? How does your parent say your name when you're in trouble? How does a sibling or classmate say your name when they're teasing you?

It's great to hear your name spoken by someone who loves you and is happy with you. It's not great to hear your name spoken by someone who is angry or who doesn't care about your feelings.

How do you say God's name? Is it with love? respect? care? meanness? God can hear you when you say His name. When we use His name without care or love, we are sinning.

When we sin, we can pray and call on the name of Jesus, our Savior. Because Jesus paid for all your sins, God the Father will forgive you. He loves you and calls you by name to be His child.

Think and Share

How do you speak about God's Word? Do you study it and speak about it as the truth?

What is one way you honor God's name? How do people dishonor God's name?

How can you honor your heavenly Father's name today?

Sing

Lord, Keep Us Steadfast in Your Word (*LSB* 655:1; *OAR* 264:1)

> Lord, keep us steadfast in Your Word; Curb those who by deceit or sword
> Would wrest the kingdom from Your Son And bring to naught all He
> has done.

Bible Memory Verse

Let him who has My word speak My word faithfully. (Jeremiah 23:28)

Pray

Dear heavenly Father, help me to honor Your name and keep it holy by speaking and teaching only what Your Word says, and by living a life that honors You and Your Word.

SECOND PETITION

Thy kingdom come.

What does this mean?
The kingdom of God certainly comes by itself without our prayer, but we pray in this petition that it may come to us also.

How does God's kingdom come?
God's kingdom comes when our heavenly Father gives us His Holy Spirit, so that by His grace we believe His holy Word and lead godly lives here in time and there in eternity.

Understanding the Second Petition

- The kingdom of God is God's loving and gracious rule over His people.
- All who believe in the Gospel of Jesus Christ belong to God's kingdom.
- As our eternal King, Jesus rules us with grace and love and gives us His Spirit to help us live lives that are pleasing to Him.
- We pray that the kingdom of God comes to us and to all people as the Spirit works through the Word.

THE MAIN IDEA
Jesus is my King. Everyone who believes in Him is part of His heavenly kingdom. We pray that God would give us and all people His Spirit so that we believe the Gospel and live God-pleasing lives. We look forward to the day Jesus returns and we will see His kingdom in all its glory.

Learning about the Second Petition

What is the kingdom of God?

- The kingdom of God is the gracious rule and reign of God.
- The kingdom of God was promised in the Old Testament and began when Jesus entered our world.
- We live in the kingdom of God now as Jesus rules over His people with love, mercy, and grace.
- We will see God's kingdom in all its glory when Jesus returns.

2 Samuel 7:12, 16 [God made this promise to David:] "When your days are fulfilled and you lie down with your fathers, I will raise up your offspring after you, who shall come from your body, and I will establish his kingdom. . . . And your house and your kingdom shall be made sure forever before Me. Your throne shall be established forever."

Mark 1:15 [Jesus said,] "The time is fulfilled, and the kingdom of God is at hand; repent and believe in the gospel."

John 3:5 Jesus answered, "Truly, truly, I say to you, unless one is born of water and the Spirit, he cannot enter the kingdom of God."

Revelation 11:15 Then the seventh angel blew his trumpet, and there were loud voices in heaven, saying, "The kingdom of the world has become the kingdom of our Lord and of His Christ, and He shall reign forever and ever."

What are we asking our Father for in this petition?

As we ask for God's kingdom to be here with us, we pray that

- God would give us His Spirit so that we can live under His loving rule and serve Him;
- the Spirit would bring others to His kingdom through the Word; and
- Jesus would return soon so that we can live in His perfect kingdom of glory.

Isaiah 55:11 So shall My word be that goes out from My mouth; it shall not return to Me empty, but it shall accomplish that which I purpose, and shall succeed in the thing for which I sent it.

Matthew 9:38 Therefore pray earnestly to the Lord of the harvest to send out laborers into His harvest.

A Bible Illustration

Pilate did not understand that Jesus' kingdom was not an earthly kingdom. Read about it in John 18:33–40.

What question did Pilate ask Jesus, and what was Jesus' answer?

What kind of King is Jesus?

Faith Connections

What is something you're really looking forward to? Your birthday? Christmas? Summer break? How do you feel when that time finally comes?

God's people had been looking forward to the coming of the Savior for a long time. When Jesus came, He announced, "The time is fulfilled, and the kingdom of God is at hand" (Mark 1:15). Through faith in Jesus, we live under God in His kingdom today. But our waiting isn't over. We are waiting for the day when Jesus will come again to cast out the devil and his kingdom forever, so only the perfect, eternal kingdom of God remains. What an awesome day that will be!

 ## Think and Share

What's the most exciting thing you've ever looked forward to? What do you think it will be like when Jesus comes again?

God wants all people to live under Him in His kingdom. Who can you tell about Jesus, your King? What will you say about Him?

 ## Sing

A Mighty Fortress Is Our God (*LSB* 656:4)
> The Word they still shall let remain Nor any thanks have for it;
> He's by our side upon the plain With His good gifts and Spirit.
> And take they our life, Goods, fame, child, and wife,
> Though these all be gone, Our vict'ry has been won;
> The Kingdom ours remaineth.

 ## Bible Memory Verse

Jesus answered, "Truly, truly, I say to you, unless one is born of water and the Spirit, he cannot enter the kingdom of God." (John 3:5)

 ## Pray

Dear Jesus, You are my King! Thank You for bringing me to faith by the Gospel so that I can live in Your kingdom. Thank You for ruling over me and all believers with grace and love. Send Your Holy Spirit so other people will also believe and live in Your kingdom. Amen.

Thy will be done on earth as it is in heaven.

What does this mean?
The good and gracious will of God is done even without our prayer, but we pray in this petition that it may be done among us also.

How is God's will done?
God's will is done when He breaks and hinders every evil plan and purpose of the devil, the world, and our sinful nature, which do not want us to hallow God's name or let His kingdom come; and when He strengthens and keeps us firm in His Word and faith until we die. This is His good and gracious will.

Understanding the Third Petition

- God's will is that all people believe in Jesus Christ as their Savior and are saved.

- We pray that God would not allow the evil plans of the devil, the world, or our sinful selves to slow the spread of the Gospel or keep people from believing in Jesus.

- We pray that God stops the devil's plans and strengthens us with His Word so that we stay faithful, even when we suffer.

- God's will for me is that I live as His child through faith in Jesus.

> **THE MAIN IDEA**
> The will of God is that all people believe in Jesus as their Savior and are saved. We pray that God would not allow the devil, the world, and our sinful selves to take us away from God and our faith in Him.

Learning about the Third Petition

What is the will of God?

God's will is that all people come to know Him as their Father and believe in Jesus Christ as their Savior.

John 6:40 For this is the will of My Father, that everyone who looks on the Son and believes in Him should have eternal life, and I will raise him up on the last day.

What do we pray for in this petition?

We ask that God would stop every evil plan of the devil, the world, or our sinful selves that would take away our faith in Jesus.

1 Peter 5:8 Be sober-minded; be watchful. Your adversary the devil prowls around like a roaring lion, seeking someone to devour.

How does God do this?

God prevents the devil from carrying out his evil plans and strengthens us with His Word so that we can stay faithful, even when we suffer.

2 Thessalonians 3:3 But the Lord is faithful. He will establish you and guard you against the evil one.

Will the devil be defeated forever?

Jesus Christ already *defeated* (won victory over) the devil through His life, death, and resurrection. When Jesus returns, the devil will be sent away and his power over us will be destroyed forever.

Romans 16:20 The God of peace will soon crush Satan under your feet. The grace of our Lord Jesus Christ be with you.

What is God's will for my life?

- God wants me to become and stay His child through faith in Jesus;
- He wants me to live as His child by following His Word and sharing it; and
- God wants me to *resist* (fight against) the devil and anything that would take me away from God.

A Bible Illustration

Even though Jesus knew how much He would suffer on the cross, He prayed for His Father's will to be done. Read about it in Matthew 26:36–46.

What was Jesus' prayer to His Father in heaven?

What was the will of the Father for Jesus?

Faith Connections

"I know this dollar is for the offering, but I really want a soda." "Why can't I watch that PG-13 movie? Ian's mom let him watch it." "I don't feel like going to church today. Can't we just stay home?"

We often want to do things our way, don't we? It can be hard to do what others want us to do, even when we know it's something that God wants us to do. It's a problem we've had since the very first sin of Adam and Eve.

But what is God's will? God's will is that everyone would look to Jesus and believe in Him as their Savior. God's will is that all people have eternal life and live with Him forever in heaven. God's will is that we would live as His children.

That doesn't sound so bad, does it? In fact, it sounds wonderful. God loves us and He knows what is best for us. His Word will lead us in the right direction and help us to make good choices. When we pray for God's will to be done, we are praying that He will keep us close to Him and bring us to Himself one day in heaven.

 ## Think and Share

Think about a time when you wanted your way instead of God's way. What happened?

Why is God's will and way the best way?

 ## Sing

I Am Trusting Thee, Lord Jesus (*LSB* 729:6)
>I am trusting Thee, Lord Jesus; Never let me fall.
>I am trusting Thee forever And for all.

 ## Bible Memory Verse

[God] desires all people to be saved and to come to the knowledge of the truth. (1 Timothy 2:4)

 ## Pray

Dear God, You want all people to believe in Jesus and be saved. Guard me and all people against the attacks of the devil. Strengthen my faith through the Spirit and Your Word so that I also trust and believe in You. Help me to always pray, "Thy will be done." In Jesus' name I pray. Amen.

FOURTH PETITION

Give us this day our daily bread.

What does this mean?
God certainly gives daily bread to everyone without our prayers, even to all evil people, but we pray in this petition that God would lead us to realize this and to receive our daily bread with thanksgiving.

What is meant by daily bread?
Daily bread includes everything that has to do with the support and needs of the body, such as food, drink, clothing, shoes, house, home, land, animals, money, goods, a devout husband or wife, devout children, devout workers, devout and faithful rulers, good government, good weather, peace, health, self-control, good reputation, good friends, faithful neighbors, and the like.

Understanding the Fourth Petition

- Daily bread is everything we need to live.
- Every good thing that we have comes from God.
- We pray that we look to God for everything we need and remember that He is the one who gives us all we need.
- We pray that we do not worry, but trust God for all we need, and that we are happy and satisfied with what He gives us.

> **THE MAIN IDEA**
> God gives us all that we need to live each day. We pray that we would know and remember that God is the one who gives us every good thing, and to thank Him for all His gifts.

- We are to share the blessings that God has given to us with others.

Learning about the Fourth Petition

What do we mean by "daily bread"?

The Bible uses *bread* to talk about everything that we need to live. *Daily* reminds us how every day we depend on God to give us all we need.

Psalm 104:27–29 These all look to You, to give them their food in due season. When You give it to them, they gather it up; when You open Your hand, they are filled with good things. When You hide Your face, they are dismayed; when You take away their breath, they die and return to their dust.

What do we pray for in this petition?

We pray that

- we would look to God for everything we need and not worry about the future;
- we thank God for everything He has given to us; and
- we are *content* (happy and satisfied) with what we have.

1 Peter 5:6–7   Humble yourselves, . . . casting all your anxieties on Him, because He cares for you.

Psalm 106:1   Give thanks to the LORD, for He is good, for His steadfast love endures forever!

How does God provide for our needs (daily bread)?

God gives us our daily bread through the food that the earth produces and the opportunity to work for the things we need.

Psalm 104:14   You cause the grass to grow for the livestock and plants for man to cultivate, that he may bring forth food from the earth.

2 Thessalonians 3:10, 12   For even when we were with you, we would give you this command: If anyone is not willing to work, let him not eat. . . . Now such persons we command and encourage in the Lord Jesus Christ to do their work quietly and to earn their own living.

How can we show thankfulness to God for the blessings He gives us?

We are to look to God and trust in Him for everything that we need and worship Him as the giver of every good gift. We are also to share with others in need and pray for them.

A Bible Illustration

The people of Israel were hungry. They could have trusted in the God who rescued them from slavery, but instead, they chose to complain. What would God do? Read about it in Exodus 16:1–21.

What did the people of Israel forget about God?

How did God show His love and care to the Israelites?

Faith Connections

The Israelites' stomachs grumbled. They were hungry. God had led them out of slavery in Egypt, but now they had no food. "Why, Moses? Why did you bring us here?" They were really grumbling against God. They didn't trust in God to take care of them. They forgot about all the ways that God had already blessed them.

Sometimes we grumble too, don't we? "Why can't I stay up late?" "Why can't my hair be curly instead of straight?" "Why do we have to have meat loaf—*again*?" When we grumble, we forget about all God's blessings. God blesses us each day with food, clothes, a loving family and friends, and the greatest blessing of all: forgiveness and new life in Jesus. So the next time you feel like grumbling, say a thank-You prayer to God instead. He will help you be happy with what you have!

 ## Think and Share

What are your "daily needs"? See how many you can write down in one minute.

Mealtime is an especially good time to remember to thank God for all His blessings. What is your favorite mealtime prayer?

 ## Sing

Feed Thy Children, God Most Holy (*LSB* 774:1)
> Feed Thy children, God most holy; Comfort sinners poor and lowly.
> O Thou Bread of Life from heaven, Bless the food Thou here hast given!
> As these gifts the body nourish, May our souls in graces flourish
> Till with saints in heavn'ly splendor At Thy feast due thanks we render.

 ## Bible Memory Verse

> The eyes of all look to You, and You give them their food in due season.
> (Psalm 145:15)

 ## Pray

Dear God, You love to give good gifts to Your children! Thank You for the many blessings that You give to me each day. Help me to remember to pray to You for all that I need. Help me pray for the needs of others too. Send Your Spirit to help me share what I have with others. In Jesus' name I pray. Amen.

And forgive us our trespasses as we forgive those who trespass against us.

What does this mean?

We pray in this petition that our Father in heaven would not look at our sins, or deny our prayer because of them. We are neither worthy of the things for which we pray, nor have we deserved them, but we ask that He would give them all to us by grace, for we daily sin much and surely deserve nothing but punishment. So we too will sincerely forgive and gladly do good to those who sin against us.

Understanding the Fifth Petition

- *Trespasses* are sins.

- We sin every day and deserve punishment.

- Our sins keep us away from our perfect God.

- Jesus died on the cross to take the punishment for our sins. He offers forgiveness to all who believe in Him.

- We pray for God to forgive our sins and to help us forgive others.

> **THE MAIN IDEA**
> We pray that God would forgive our sins for Jesus' sake and help us to forgive those who sin against us.

Learning about the Fifth Petition

What do we pray for in this petition?

We ask that our Father in heaven would forgive our sins for Jesus' sake.

Psalm 51:1–2   Have mercy on me, O God, according to Your steadfast love; according to Your abundant mercy blot out my transgressions. Wash me thoroughly from my iniquity, and cleanse me from my sin!

Why do we need to pray for God to forgive us?

- We sin every day. We deserve punishment for our sins.

- Our sins *separate* us (keep us away) from our perfect God.

- Jesus' forgiveness gives us peace with God.

Psalm 32:1, 5   Blessed is the one whose transgression is forgiven, whose sin is covered. . . . I acknowledged my sin to You, and I did not cover my iniquity; I said, "I will confess my transgressions to the LORD," and You forgave the iniquity of my sin.

Why is forgiveness important for my own life?

Because God has forgiven my sins, now I can forgive others who sin against me. When I forgive others, I let go of my anger and hatred toward them.

Romans 3:23–24   For all have sinned and fall short of the glory of God, and are justified by His grace as a gift, through the redemption that is in Christ Jesus.

Ephesians 4:32   Be kind to one another, tenderhearted, forgiving one another, as God in Christ forgave you.

Does God's forgiveness depend on whether we choose to forgive others?

No. We can't earn God's forgiveness. God's forgiveness is a free gift from Him. God forgives us because Jesus paid the punishment for our sins. God's forgiveness of our sins gives us strength to forgive other people who sin against us.

Colossians 3:13   Bearing with one another and, if one has a complaint against another, forgiving each other; as the Lord has forgiven you, so you also must forgive.

A Bible Illustration

Joseph's brothers had treated him badly. They had even sold him as a slave! How would Joseph treat them when they came to him in Egypt many years later? Read about it in Genesis 45:1–15.

What did Joseph say to his brothers?

Why do you think that Joseph was able to forgive his brothers for the terrible things they had done to him?

Faith Connections

"I'll never, ever forgive you!" Have you ever heard someone say that? Have you ever said it yourself? It can be hard to forgive when someone has been very mean to you. But that's exactly what God wants us to do!

Joseph's brothers had been very mean to him. Now that Joseph was an important ruler in Egypt, he could get back at his brothers and punish them! But that's not what Joseph did. Instead, he forgave them.

God has every reason to punish us for our sins. We disobey His Commandments and hurt others with our sins every day. But instead of punishing us, God forgives us. Jesus took the punishment for our sins so that we can be forgiven. And because God has forgiven you, He helps you to forgive others!

 ## Think and Share

How was Joseph able to forgive his brothers?

How are you able to forgive people who sin against you?

 ## Sing

Chief of Sinners Though I Be (*LSB* 611:3)
> Only Jesus can impart Balm to heal the wounded heart,
> Peace that flows from sin forgiv'n, Joy that lifts the soul to heav'n,
> Faith and hope to walk with God In the way that Enoch trod.

 ## Bible Memory Verse

If we confess our sins, He is faithful and just to forgive us our sins and to cleanse us from all unrighteousness. (1 John 1:9)

 ## Pray

Dear God, I confess that I sin every day when I disobey Your Commandments and hurt others with my words and actions. Please forgive me for Jesus' sake. Help me to forgive the people who sin against me. Thank You for Your great love for me and all people! In Jesus' name I pray. Amen.

SIXTH PETITION

And lead us not into temptation.

What does this mean?

God tempts no one. We pray in this petition that God would guard and keep us so that the devil, the world, and our sinful nature may not deceive us or mislead us into false belief, despair, and other great shame and vice. Although we are attacked by these things, we pray that we may finally overcome them and win the victory.

Understanding the Sixth Petition

- Our enemies—the devil, the world, and our sinful selves—try to lead us away from God into sin and unbelief.

- We pray that God would guard us against temptations and evils that would harm or take away our faith.

- God helps us fight against the temptation to sin by giving us His Word, His Spirit, and prayer.

> **THE MAIN IDEA**
> We pray that God would guard and protect us against the sins that come from the devil, the world, and our sinful selves, and that He would keep us strong in faith and in our love for Jesus.

Learning about the Sixth Petition

What do we pray in this petition?

We pray that God would

- keep us strong in faith and in our love for Jesus, our Savior;

- help us be on guard against evils that would harm or take away our faith; and

- guard us against the temptations to sin that come from the devil, the world, and our own sinful selves.

1 Peter 5:8–9 Be sober-minded; be watchful. Your adversary the devil prowls around like a roaring lion, seeking someone to devour. Resist him, firm in your faith, knowing that the same kinds of suffering are being experienced by your brotherhood throughout the world.

Mark 14:38 Watch and pray that you may not enter into temptation. The spirit indeed is willing, but the flesh is weak.

How does God help us fight against temptations?

God gives us the gifts of His Word, the Holy Spirit, Baptism, forgiveness, and prayer to help us fight against threats to our faith and the temptation to sin.

Ephesians 6:11, 17–18 Put on the whole armor of God, that you may be able to stand against the schemes of the devil. . . . And take the helmet of salvation, and the sword of the Spirit, which is the word of God, praying at all times in the Spirit, with all prayer and supplication. To that end, keep alert with all perseverance, making supplication for all the saints.

1 Corinthians 10:13 No temptation has overtaken you that is not common to man. God is faithful, and He will not let you be tempted beyond your ability, but with the temptation He will also provide the way of escape, that you may be able to endure it.

Does God ever tempt us?

No. God does not tempt us to sin. However, sometimes God tests our faith when He allows difficult times in our lives. God does this to strengthen our faith and bring us closer to Him.

James 1:13 Let no one say when he is tempted, "I am being tempted by God," for God cannot be tempted with evil, and He Himself tempts no one.

James 1:2–3 Count it all joy, my brothers, when you meet trials of various kinds, for you know that the testing of your faith produces steadfastness.

A Bible Illustration

The devil tempted Adam and Eve to disobey God and eat fruit from the tree that God had told them not to eat from. Read about it in Genesis 3:1–13.

What did the serpent (the devil) say to Eve to tempt her to eat the fruit?

What happened after Adam and Eve ate the fruit?

Faith Connections

Mom said no cookies before dinner. But Mom's not in the kitchen—she'll never notice if you take just one. Your brother's wallet is sitting open on the table. He won't mind if you "borrow" a dollar without asking, will he? Your friends are whispering about the new girl in your class. You know you should go and say "Hi" to her, but it would be so much easier to join in with your friends.

Temptations! Every day the devil, other people, and even our own sinful selves tempt us to do things that we know are wrong. Jesus knew we would face temptations; He faced them too! So Jesus taught us to pray, "Lead us not into temptation." When we're tempted to do something wrong, we can pray to God to help us do what is right instead. He promises to help us. What a loving God we have!

 ## Think and Share

Think about a time when you were tempted to do something wrong. What did you do? How does God help us fight temptation?

 ## Sing

What a Friend We Have in Jesus (*LSB* 770:2; *OAR* 287:2)
> Have we trials and temptations? Is there trouble anywhere?
> We should never be discouraged—Take it to the Lord in prayer.
> Can we find a friend so faithful Who will all our sorrows share?
> Jesus knows our ev'ry weakness—Take it to the Lord in prayer.

 ## Bible Memory Verse

Be sober-minded; be watchful. Your adversary the devil prowls around like a roaring lion, seeking someone to devour. Resist him, firm in your faith. (1 Peter 5:8–9)

 ## Pray

Heavenly Father, when the devil and the world tempt me to sin, help me keep from sinning. Protect me from the things that would lead me away from You. Strengthen my faith in Jesus as my Savior, and keep me close to You. In Jesus' name I pray. Amen.

But deliver us from evil.

What does this mean?
We pray in this petition, in summary, that our Father in heaven would rescue us from every evil of body and soul, possessions and reputation, and finally, when our last hour comes, give us a blessed end, and graciously take us from this valley of sorrow to Himself in heaven.

Understanding the Seventh Petition

- We pray that God would protect and guard us from the many evils in this life.
- We pray that God would help us endure the troubles of life and keep us faithful to Him our whole lives.
- This petition sums up all the requests of the Lord's Prayer: we pray that our Father in heaven would rescue us from all evil, including the devil.

> **THE MAIN IDEA**
> We pray that God would protect and rescue us from the devil and from all evil, both now and forever.

Learning about the Seventh Petition

What do we pray in this petition?

We ask God to

- keep us from the many evils in life, such as sickness, hurt, and deep sadness;
- help us endure the troubles that come to us, and keep us strong in faith; and
- keep us faithful to Him and take us to Himself when we die.

Psalm 59:1   Deliver me from my enemies, O my God; protect me from those who rise up against me.

Galatians 1:4–5   [Christ] gave Himself for our sins to deliver us from the present evil age, according to the will of our God and Father, to whom be the glory forever and ever. Amen.

What do we know about the devil, Satan?

The devil is God's enemy, the evil one. Satan was created a holy angel, but he rebelled against God. The devil hates God and all that is good. He wants to take all people away from God.

> **Revelation 12:9**   And the great dragon was thrown down, that ancient serpent, who is called the devil and Satan, the deceiver of the whole world—he was thrown down to the earth, and his angels were thrown down with him.

> **Isaiah 14:12–15**   How you are fallen from heaven, O Day Star, son of Dawn! How you are cut down to the ground, you who laid the nations low! You said in your heart, "I will ascend to heaven; above the stars of God I will set my throne on high; I will sit on the mount of assembly in the far reaches of the north; I will ascend above the heights of the clouds; I will make myself like the Most High." But you are brought down to Sheol, to the far reaches of the pit.

What hope do we have in the battle against the devil?

Our hope is in Jesus Christ, who won the victory over the devil through His death and resurrection. Through faith in Jesus, we also have victory over the devil.

> **Colossians 1:11–14**   May you be strengthened with all power, according to His glorious might, for all endurance and patience with joy, giving thanks to the Father, who has qualified you to share in the inheritance of the saints in light. He has delivered us from the domain of darkness and transferred us to the kingdom of His beloved Son, in whom we have redemption, the forgiveness of sins.

A Bible Illustration

Evil men made a plan to trap faithful Daniel, but God helped Daniel stay faithful to Him, and He rescued Daniel from danger. Read about it in Daniel 6.

What evil did the high officials plan against Daniel?

How did God keep Daniel from evil?

Faith Connections

Think of your favorite superhero movie. Often, the "bad guy" has an evil plan to hurt people or take over the world. The hero steps in to protect and save the people.

Of course, these movies aren't real. But evil is real. The real "bad guy" is the devil, who tries to destroy God's good world and take people away from Him.

Jesus taught us to pray, "Deliver us from evil." As long as we live in this sin-filled world, we will face evils like sin, sickness, pain, sadness, and even death. But the power of those things is nothing compared to the power of our God. When we face evil, Jesus tells us to go to our heavenly Father in prayer, asking Him to protect us, strengthen us, and deliver us from the evil one. He promises He will help us! We don't need to be afraid, because we know that Jesus has already defeated the devil.

 ## Think and Share

Who's your favorite superhero? What is so special about him or her? Now think about God. What is the most amazing, special thing about our Savior God?

 ## Sing

A Mighty Fortress Is Our God (*LSB* 656:3; *OAR* 262:3)
> Though devils all the world should fill, All eager to devour us,
> We tremble not, we fear no ill; They shall not overpow'r us.
> This world's prince may still Scowl fierce as he will,
> He can harm us none. He's judged; the deed is done;
> One little word can fell him.

 ## Bible Memory Verse

The Lord will keep you from all evil; He will keep your life. The Lord will keep your going out and your coming in from this time forth and forevermore. (Psalm 121:7–8)

 ## Pray

Heavenly Father, sometimes I feel a little worried or afraid when I see the evil in this world. Help me to trust in You and pray, "Deliver us from evil." Help me remember that You already won the victory over evil when Jesus died and rose again. Send Your Spirit to keep my faith in You strong all my life. Amen.

CONCLUSION

For Thine is the kingdom and the power and the glory forever and ever. Amen.

What does this mean?

This means that I should be certain that these petitions are pleasing to our Father in heaven, and are heard by Him; for He Himself has commanded us to pray in this way and has promised to hear us. Amen, amen means "yes, yes, it shall be so."

Understanding the Conclusion

- We know the words of this prayer are pleasing to God, since He Himself gave these words to us to pray (see Matthew 6:9–13).

- We believe that God our Father is able to do everything that we ask of Him in the Lord's Prayer.

- God has commanded us to pray, and He has promised to hear us.

> **THE MAIN IDEA**
> We close the Lord's Prayer by praising God our Father as the one who is able to do everything that we ask.

Learning about the Conclusion

Why did the Early Church include these words at the end of the Lord's Prayer?

These words declare that we believe that God our Father is able to do everything that we ask in this prayer. God our Father

- is the King who gives us every good gift;

- has the power to do what we ask of Him; and

- is praised as the one true God.

1 Chronicles 29:11 Yours, O LORD, is the greatness and the power and the glory and the victory and the majesty, for all that is in the heavens and in the earth is Yours. Yours is the kingdom, O LORD, and You are exalted as head above all.

James 1:17   Every good gift and every perfect gift is from above, coming down from the Father of lights, with whom there is no variation or shadow due to change.

Ephesians 3:20–21   Now to Him who is able to do far more abundantly than all that we ask or think, according to the power at work within us, to Him be glory in the church and in Christ Jesus throughout all generations, forever and ever. Amen.

1 Timothy 1:17   To the King of the ages, immortal, invisible, the only God, be honor and glory forever and ever. Amen.

Why do we end the Lord's Prayer with the word Amen?

Amen is a word from the Old Testament that means "so shall it be." We are certain that God will hear our prayers, for He has commanded us to pray them; and He will answer our prayers, for He has promised to hear us when we pray.

1 Chronicles 16:36   "Blessed be the LORD, the God of Israel, from everlasting to everlasting!" Then all the people said, "Amen!" and praised the LORD.

A Bible Illustration

Jesus taught the people to ask their heavenly Father for the things they needed, just as a person in need asks a friend, or children ask their father. Read Luke 11:5–13.

What kinds of gifts do earthly fathers give their children?

What kinds of gifts does our heavenly Father give to us?

Faith Connections

We usually end a story with "The End." We usually end a prayer with "Amen." Do they mean the same thing? Not really. In fact, in a way, "Amen" starts something new. *Amen* means "Yes! This is true." It's a way of saying you believe God's promise to hear and answer you. You trust He knows what is best for you. So while an "Amen" can end a prayer, it does not end the conversation between you and God. God will still work. He will speak to you in His Word. You will continue to live your life prayerfully with the help of the Holy Spirit. You know that God the Father listens to you as a father listens to his child.

A story might end with "The End," but the story might not be true. When we pray according to God's Word and trusting in His promises, your "Amen! This is true!" can be certain.

Think and Share

When do you pray the Lord's Prayer? When do you pray other prayers?

How does it feel to know that God promises to hear your prayers?

The next time you pray "Amen," say it boldly and with joy! "Yes, yes, this is true!"

Sing

Our Father, Who from Heaven Above (*LSB* 766:9; *OAR* 354:9)
> Amen, that is, so shall it be. Make strong our faith in You, that we
> May doubt not but with trust believe That what we ask we shall receive.
> Thus in Your name and at Your Word We say, "Amen, O hear us, Lord!"

Bible Memory Verse

> The LORD is high above all nations, and His glory above the heavens! Who is like the LORD our God, who is seated on high[?] (Psalm 113:4–5)

Pray

Dear God, thank You for the gift of prayer. I can talk to the God of all things—anytime! Thank You for promising to hear me and for promising to answer in the best way for me. Help me to turn to You in prayer anytime I need to talk to You. You have all the power and glory. Amen!

Introduction to the Sacrament of Holy Baptism

God has given Baptism as a gift to His people. Through Baptism, by faith, God gives us the forgiveness of sins, new life, and salvation. In Baptism, God brings us into His family as His precious children.

- A sacrament is a holy act commanded by God that has an earthly element combined with God's Word and that offers the forgiveness of sins earned by Jesus Christ.

- Jesus Christ, our Lord, commanded His Church to baptize all nations. This means that infants and little children should also be baptized.

- In Baptism, God puts His saving name on us, and we become His children.

- In Baptism, God works through water and His Word to forgive our sins, rescue us from death and the devil, and give us eternal salvation.

First

What is Baptism?
**Baptism is not just plain water, but it
is the water included in God's command and combined with God's word.**

Which is that word of God?
**Christ our Lord says in the last chapter of Matthew: "Therefore go
and make disciples of all nations, baptizing them in the name of the
Father and of the Son and of the Holy Spirit." (Matt. 28:19)**

Understanding the Nature of Baptism

- Baptism is a sacrament in which God forgives our sins through water and His Word.

- In Baptism, God puts His saving name on us, and we become His children.

- Jesus commanded "all nations" to be baptized: every man, woman, child, and baby in every nation of the world.

> **THE MAIN IDEA**
> In Baptism, God forgives our sins and makes us His children through water and His Word.

Learning about the Nature of Baptism

What is Baptism?

- Baptism is a *sacrament* (a holy act commanded by God that has an earthly element combined with God's Word and that offers the forgiveness of sins earned by Jesus Christ).

- In Baptism, God gives forgiveness of sins to the person being baptized with water and in the name of the Father, Son, and Holy Spirit.

- Jesus commanded and *instituted* (began or established) Baptism.

Matthew 28:18–20 [Jesus said,] "All authority in heaven and on earth has been given to Me. Go therefore and make disciples of all nations, baptizing them in the name of the Father and of the Son and of the Holy Spirit, teaching them to observe all that I have commanded you. And behold, I am with you always, to the end of the age."

What does the word baptize mean?

- *Baptize* means "to wash with water." This washing can be through *immersing* (covering completely in water), pouring, or sprinkling.
- In Christian Baptism, water is applied to a person in the name of the Father, Son, and Holy Spirit.
- God *washes away* (forgives) our sins in Baptism.

Ephesians 5:25–26   Christ loved the church and gave Himself up for her, that He might sanctify her, having cleansed her by the washing of water with the word.

What does it mean to be baptized "in the name of the Father and of the Son and of the Holy Spirit"?

To be baptized in God's name means that it is God doing the work. In Baptism, God puts His saving name on us, and we become His children.

Exodus 20:24   In every place where I cause My name to be remembered I will come to you and bless you.

Who should be baptized?

Jesus commanded His Church to baptize "all nations." This includes every man, woman, child, and baby in every nation of the world—everyone.

Acts 2:38–39   Repent and be baptized every one of you in the name of Jesus Christ for the forgiveness of your sins, and you will receive the gift of the Holy Spirit. For the promise is for you and for your children and for all who are far off, everyone whom the Lord our God calls to Himself.

A Bible Illustration

After an earthquake shook the jail, the jailer asked Paul and Silas, "What must I do to be saved?" Read what happened next in Acts 16:25–34.

What did Paul and Silas tell the jailer?

Whom did Paul and Silas baptize that night?

Faith Connections

Imagine that you are on a field trip to a farm. You're on a hayride when it starts pouring down rain and the tractor gets stuck. As you're getting off the tractor into the muddy field, you slip! You fall facedown in the mud. You're filthy. And stinky. You're a mess. All you can think about is taking a nice warm shower to get clean!

Now think about life. We know God's Commandments, what He wants us to do, but we slip up. We lie, cheat, or think bad thoughts. We sin. Every time we sin, it's like a fall in the mud. Our sins cover us like that dirty mud. How can we ever get clean? Taking a bath or a shower won't do it. Only Jesus can wash away our sins. In Baptism, God washes away our sins and makes us His forgiven children. Every day, God keeps washing away the sins of His baptized children, for Jesus' sake.

Think and Share

Ask your parents or caregivers to tell you about your Baptism. When and where were you baptized? Who are your sponsors? Celebrate your Baptism birthday!

Sing

Go and Baptize All the Nations (*OAR* 349:2)
> By the Word and in the water, All our sins are washed away.
> Faith and life and God's protection All are ours in this new day.
> This event is not our doing. It is all God's blessed grace.
> What a wonder! We are children Who will see the Father's face!

Bible Memory Verse

Go therefore and make disciples of all nations, baptizing them in the name of the Father and of the Son and of the Holy Spirit, teaching them to observe all that I have commanded you. And behold, I am with you always, to the end of the age. (Matthew 28:19–20)

Pray

I thank You, my heavenly Father, that through Baptism You have washed me clean of all my sins and have made me Your child. Help me remember everything that You have done for me in my Baptism. Send Your Spirit to keep me always faithful to You. In Jesus' name I pray. Amen.

Second

What benefits does Baptism give?
It works forgiveness of sins, rescues from death and the devil, and gives eternal salvation to all who believe this, as the words and promises of God declare.

Which are these words and promises of God?
Christ our Lord says in the last chapter of Mark: "Whoever believes and is baptized will be saved, but whoever does not believe will be condemned." (Mark 16:16)

Understanding the Blessings of Baptism

- In Baptism, God forgives our sins, rescues us from death and the devil, and gives us eternal life.

- In Baptism, we personally receive the forgiveness of sins Jesus won for the world.

- In Baptism, we have God's sure promise that He has forgiven our sins and rescued us from death and the devil.

> **THE MAIN IDEA**
> God promises wonderful gifts in Baptism: the Holy Spirit, the forgiveness of sins, and eternal life with Him in heaven.

Learning about the Blessings of Baptism

What great things does God do through Baptism?

- God forgives our sins.

- God rescues us from death and the devil.

- God gives us eternal life.

Acts 2:38   Peter said to them, "Repent and be baptized every one of you in the name of Jesus Christ for the forgiveness of your sins, and you will receive the gift of the Holy Spirit."

Romans 6:3–5   Do you not know that all of us who have been baptized into Christ Jesus were baptized into His death? We were buried therefore with Him by baptism into death, in order that, just as Christ was raised from the dead by the glory of the Father, we too might walk in newness of life. For if we have been united with Him in a death like His, we shall certainly be united with Him in a resurrection like His.

Why do we need to be baptized?

Jesus commanded us to be baptized. Through Baptism, Jesus Christ gives to each person the forgiveness of sins that He won for the whole world.

1 Corinthians 6:11   But you were washed, you were sanctified, you were justified in the name of the Lord Jesus Christ and by the Spirit of our God.

Can an unbaptized person be saved?

Yes. Only those who do not believe in Jesus as their Savior will not be saved. However, those who have faith in Jesus will want to obey His command to be baptized and have their children baptized and receive the blessings that Baptism gives.

Mark 16:16   Whoever believes and is baptized will be saved, but whoever does not believe will be condemned.

How does Baptism help me now and when I die?

In Baptism, we have God's promise that He has forgiven our sins and rescued us from death and the devil. In times of trouble, and when we face death, we can say with confidence, "I am baptized into Christ" and be comforted that we are God's forgiven children.

Romans 8:1   There is therefore now no condemnation for those who are in Christ Jesus.

A Bible Illustration

On Pentecost, Peter preached the Good News about Jesus' life, death, and resurrection to the crowd. Read about how the crowd responded in Acts 2:37–41.

What did Peter tell the crowd that they should do?

What gifts would the people receive when they were baptized?

Faith Connections

Have you ever thought about Baptism being sticky? That might sound strange. After all, water isn't sticky! It usually washes away sticky things. But in Baptism, Jesus "sticks" to you—kind of like glue! Jesus was baptized. You were baptized. Jesus was tempted (and did not sin). You are tempted (and do sin). Jesus died. You will probably die. Jesus rose—and guess what! You will rise! Because you are connected to Jesus, you follow Him, even right into heaven and eternal life.

We can thank Jesus for doing everything for us, only perfectly. Because He did everything right for us, we can enjoy the blessings that His perfect life brings: holiness, life, and joy, to name a few.

Think and Share

Make a sign for your room that says, "I am a baptized child of God!" Whenever you look at it, you can remember God's promises to you, given in Baptism: He has forgiven you, He has rescued you, He loves you, and you are His precious child.

Baptism makes you a child of God. Other people are baptized too. What does that mean about your relationship with them?

Sing

Baptized into Your Name Most Holy (*LSB* 590:1)
> Baptized into Your name most holy, O Father, Son, and Holy Ghost,
> I claim a place, though weak and lowly, Among Your saints, Your chosen host.
> Buried with Christ and dead to sin, Your Spirit now shall live within.

Bible Memory Verse

> Whoever believes and is baptized will be saved, but whoever does not believe will be condemned. (Mark 16:16)

Pray

Dear heavenly Father, help me remember that through Your Word, Baptism washes away my sins, rescues me from death and the devil, and gives me eternal life with You in heaven! I thank and praise You for all these blessings. In Jesus' name I pray. Amen.

Third

How can water do such great things?
Certainly not just water, but the word of God in and with the water does these things, along with the faith which trusts this word of God in the water. For without God's word the water is plain water and no Baptism. But with the word of God it is a Baptism, that is, a life-giving water, rich in grace, and a washing of the new birth in the Holy Spirit, as St. Paul says in Titus, chapter three: "He saved us through the washing of rebirth and renewal by the Holy Spirit, whom He poured out on us generously through Jesus Christ our Savior, so that, having been justified by His grace, we might become heirs having the hope of eternal life. This is a trustworthy saying." (Titus 3:5–8)

Understanding the Power of Baptism

- The power in Baptism comes from the Word of God.
- We receive the blessings of Baptism through faith.
- Through Baptism, we live a new life as God's children who are filled with the Holy Spirit.

> **THE MAIN IDEA**
> The Word of God gives Baptism the power to forgive sins, rescue from death and the devil, and give eternal life. We receive these gifts through Baptism by faith.

Learning about the Power of Baptism

How can plain water give forgiveness of sins, rescue from death and the devil, and give eternal life?

Water by itself cannot give these blessings. In Baptism, water is combined with the Word of God to give these blessings, and we receive them by faith.

Acts 2:38–39 And Peter said to them, "Repent and be baptized every one of you in the name of Jesus Christ for the forgiveness of your sins, and you will receive the gift of the Holy Spirit. For the promise is for you and for your children and for all who are far off, everyone whom the Lord our God calls to Himself."

What does it mean that Baptism is a "washing of rebirth and renewal by the Holy Spirit"?

The Holy Spirit works through Baptism to create faith in Jesus. The Spirit makes us children of God who are "reborn" in Baptism to live a new life, filled with the Spirit.

John 3:5–6   Jesus answered, "Truly, truly, I say to you, unless one is born of water and the Spirit, he cannot enter the kingdom of God. That which is born of the flesh is flesh, and that which is born of the Spirit is spirit."

2 Corinthians 5:17   Therefore, if anyone is in Christ, he is a new creation. The old has passed away; behold, the new has come.

Do I need to be baptized by the Holy Spirit in addition to my Baptism?

No. The Holy Spirit works through the one Baptism that Jesus commanded and instituted. Christian Baptism is a Baptism of water and the Holy Spirit.

Ephesians 4:5   One Lord, one faith, one baptism.

A Bible Illustration

Nicodemus wanted to know more about Jesus and His mission. Jesus told him what needed to happen in Nicodemus's life, and what He (Jesus) had come to do. Read about it in John 3:1–16.

What was Nicodemus confused about?

What did Jesus explain to Nicodemus?

Faith Connections

What's the most powerful thing you can think of? An earthquake? A flood? A lightning bolt? A superhero? There is something even more powerful than all of those put together—it's God's Word. Remember creation? God spoke, and it was. Everything came into being by God's word. The Bible is full of God's words; in fact, it *is* God's Word, all of it. When God speaks, things happen.

In Baptism, water is joined with God's Word, and things happen—wonderful things! Our sins are forgiven, we are rescued from death and the devil, and we are given the gift of eternal life with Jesus forever in heaven. We receive the gift of the Holy Spirit, and we live new lives as God's children. What a powerful God we have!

 ## Think and Share

Water can wash away dirt. What does the water of Baptism wash away?

 ## Sing

All Christians Who Have Been Baptized (*LSB* 596:4)
> In Baptism we now put on Christ—Our shame is fully covered
> With all that He once sacrificed And freely for us suffered.
> For here the flood of His own blood Now makes us holy, right, and good
> Before our heav'nly Father.

 ## Bible Memory Verse

> He saved us, not because of works done by us in righteousness, but according to His own mercy, by the washing of regeneration and renewal of the Holy Spirit. (Titus 3:5)

 ## Pray

Dear Father in heaven, thank You for saving me through water and Your powerful Word. Thank You for sending the Holy Spirit to give me new life in Baptism. Help me to always trust in You and in Your promises. I know that all Your promises are true! In Jesus' name I pray. Amen.

Fourth

What does such baptizing with water indicate?
It indicates that the Old Adam in us should by daily contrition and repentance be drowned and die with all sins and evil desires, and that a new man should daily emerge and arise to live before God in righteousness and purity forever.

Where is this written?
St. Paul writes in Romans chapter six: "We were therefore buried with Him through baptism into death in order that, just as Christ was raised from the dead through the glory of the Father, we too may live a new life." (Rom. 6:4)

Understanding What Baptism Indicates

- Every day, there is a battle going on inside of us between the "old Adam"—our sinful selves—and the "new man"—the new life that the Spirit has given to us in Baptism.

- Every day we confess our sins, putting off our sinful selves, and live a new life led by the Holy Spirit.

- We remember our Baptism with the words "in the name of the Father and of the Son and of the Holy Spirit." These words were spoken at our Baptism.

> **THE MAIN IDEA**
> As a baptized Christian, I confess my sins every day and live the new life that the Holy Spirit has created in me through Baptism.

Learning about What Baptism Indicates

What is the old Adam?

The *old Adam* (sometimes called the "old man" or "old self") is our sinful self, our desire to sin.

Ephesians 4:22 Put off your old self, which belongs to your former manner of life and is corrupt through deceitful desires.

What is the new man?

The *new man* is the new life that we live by the Spirit through Baptism. The Holy Spirit creates in us new, God-pleasing attitudes, thoughts, and actions.

2 Corinthians 5:17   Therefore, if anyone is in Christ, he is a new creation. The old has passed away; behold, the new has come.

What does the daily life of a baptized Christian look like?

Every day, we battle against temptations to sin and we confess our sins to God. And every day we ask God to help us live the new life that He has given to us, a life of God-pleasing goodness and love.

Romans 6:3–4   Do you not know that all of us who have been baptized into Christ Jesus were baptized into His death? We were buried therefore with Him by baptism into death, in order that, just as Christ was raised from the dead by the glory of the Father, we too might walk in newness of life.

What words do we use to remember our Baptism?

We remember our Baptism with the words "in the name of the Father and of the Son and of the Holy Spirit" (Matthew 28:19). We hear these words in worship (the trinitarian Invocation), and we use them in our prayers. We may make the sign of the cross as we hear these words. The sign of the cross was made at our Baptism on our foreheads and hearts to mark us as "redeemed by Christ the crucified" (*LSB*, p. 268).

A Bible Illustration

St. Paul explains how our Baptism joins us with Jesus: our old sinful self is put to death by Jesus' death, and just as Jesus was raised to life, we are also raised to new life in the Spirit. Read about it in Romans 6:3–11.

Why don't death and sin have power over baptized Christians?

Talk about what it means to "walk in newness of life" (v. 4).

Faith Connections

Do you like getting new clothes or shoes? It's fun and kind of exciting to put on something new, something that doesn't have any stains or holes or any worn-out places. Some people even like to try a "new look" by getting their hair cut differently or by dressing in a new style of clothing.

Our Baptism reminds us that every day, we need to get rid of the "old man" (our sinful self) by confessing our sins to God. Our sinful self is dirty, stained, and worn out. Then we put on the "new man," the new life that the Holy Spirit has given to us in Baptism. The new life that God gives to us is full of God-pleasing attitudes, thoughts, and actions. The Spirit gives us a "new look" that is beautiful, both to God and to the people around us!

 ## Think and Share

How do you "look different" to others as you live the new life you have been given in Baptism?

 ## Sing

All Who Believe and Are Baptized (*LSB* 601:1)
> All who believe and are baptized Shall see the Lord's salvation;
> Baptized into the death of Christ, They are a new creation.
> Through Christ's redemption they shall stand Among the glorious, heav'nly band
> Of ev'ry tribe and nation.

 ## Bible Memory Verse

We were buried therefore with Him by baptism into death, in order that, just as Christ was raised from the dead by the glory of the Father, we too might walk in newness of life. (Romans 6:4)

 ## Pray

Heavenly Father, help me each day to confess my sins and put away my sinful self. Send Your Spirit to strengthen my faith and help me live a new life that is pleasing to You. Thank You for Your promise to keep me close to You forever, as Your beloved child! In Jesus' name I pray. Amen.

Introduction to Confession
and the Office of the Keys

Every day, Christians are to confess their sins to God and receive forgiveness through Jesus Christ. The Office of the Keys is the authority Christ gives to His Church to deliver forgiveness.

- We confess our sins to God our Father, and God forgives our sins for the sake of Jesus Christ, our Savior.
- Jesus gives His Church the authority to forgive the sins of those who *repent* (feel sorrow for sin and turn away from sin) and to withhold forgiveness from those who refuse to repent of their sins.

Confession

What is Confession?

Confession has two parts. First, that we confess our sins, and second, that we receive absolution, that is, forgiveness, from the pastor as from God Himself, not doubting, but firmly believing that by it our sins are forgiven before God in heaven.

What sins should we confess?

Before God we should plead guilty of all sins, even those we are not aware of, as we do in the Lord's Prayer; but before the pastor we should confess only those sins which we know and feel in our hearts.

Which are these?

Consider your place in life according to the Ten Commandments: Are you a father, mother, son, daughter, husband, wife, or worker? Have you been disobedient, unfaithful, or lazy? Have you been hot-tempered, rude, or quarrelsome? Have you hurt someone by your words or deeds? Have you stolen, been negligent, wasted anything, or done any harm?

Understanding Confession

- When we confess our sins, we admit that we have disobeyed God's Commandments and we have not loved and trusted in Him above all things.

- The pastor speaks words of *absolution* (forgiveness) to us as a representative of Jesus. God has forgiven our sins for Jesus' sake.

> **THE MAIN IDEA**
> We confess our sins to God our Father and God forgives our sins for the sake of Jesus Christ, our Savior.

Learning about Confession

What is the first part of Confession?

We first *confess*, or admit, our sin. We confess to God that we have disobeyed His Commandments and we deserve punishment.

Psalm 32:3, 5   For when I kept silent, my bones wasted away through my groaning all day long. . . . I acknowledged my sin to You, and I did not cover my iniquity; I said, "I will confess my transgressions to the LORD," and You forgave the iniquity of my sin.

What sins should we confess to God?

We should confess all sins to God, the sins that we know we have done, and the sins that we don't even realize we have done or have forgotten. We confess the sins we meant to do, and those we did not mean to do.

1 John 1:8–9 If we say we have no sin, we deceive ourselves, and the truth is not in us. If we confess our sins, He is faithful and just to forgive us our sins and to cleanse us from all unrighteousness.

What sins should we confess to others?

We should confess to others the sins we have done against them. We ask them for forgiveness and try to make things right with them.

Matthew 5:23–24 So if you are offering your gift at the altar and there remember that your brother has something against you, leave your gift there before the altar and go. First be reconciled to your brother, and then come and offer your gift.

What is the second part of Confession?

After we have confessed our sins in worship, the pastor says, "I forgive your sins" (the Absolution). The pastor speaks with Jesus' authority and as a representative of Jesus. Therefore, we believe that God Himself has completely forgiven our sins.

John 20:23 If you forgive the sins of any, they are forgiven them; if you withhold forgiveness from any, it is withheld.

A Bible Illustration

Jesus told a parable about a Pharisee and a tax collector who both went to the temple to pray. Read about it in Luke 18:10–13.

What was the difference between the prayers of the two men?

Which man's sins were forgiven by God?

Faith Connections

There are two little words that are sometimes very hard for us to say. Those two words are "I'm sorry." When we disobey our parents or teacher, when we are unkind to a friend, when we don't do what we were told to do, we sin.

God says to us, "Confess your sins to Me. Admit that you have done wrong. Tell the person you have hurt that you are sorry." And so we say to God, "I'm sorry. I have sinned against You and against others. Please forgive me for Jesus' sake."

But it doesn't end there! God does forgive our sins, because Jesus died to take the punishment for all those sins. And so God says to you, "I forgive you, My dear child. Your sins are wiped away. Go in peace, knowing how much I love you."

What joy it is to be forgiven by our loving God!

 ## Think and Share

What have you done wrong today? What didn't you do that you should have done? Say a prayer, confessing those sins and asking God to forgive you. Then rejoice! God has forgiven you your sins, for Jesus' sake.

 ## Sing

When the Heart by Sin Is Broken (*OAR* 350:1)

> When the heart by sin is broken, When the conscience burns within,
> Let God's healing word be spoken To restore your soul again.
> Come to God with honest pleading; Ev'ry fault to Him make known.
> Trust that Christ is interceding For you at the Father's throne.

 ## Bible Memory Verse

If we say we have no sin, we deceive ourselves, and the truth is not in us. If we confess our sins, He is faithful and just to forgive us our sins and to cleanse us from all unrighteousness. (1 John 1:8–9)

 ## Pray

Heavenly Father, I am sorry that I have sinned against You and against others. Please forgive me for the sake of Your Son, Jesus, my Savior. Make my heart pure and new. Fill me with Your Spirit so that I can do Your will and walk in Your ways. Thank You for Your love and forgiveness! In Jesus' name I pray. Amen.

The Office of the Keys

What is the Office of the Keys?
The Office of the Keys is that special authority which Christ has given to His church on earth to forgive the sins of repentant sinners, but to withhold forgiveness from the unrepentant as long as they do not repent.

Where is this written?
This is what St. John the Evangelist writes in chapter twenty: The Lord Jesus breathed on His disciples and said, "Receive the Holy Spirit. If you forgive anyone his sins, they are forgiven; if you do not forgive them, they are not forgiven." (John 20:22–23)

What do you believe according to these words?
I believe that when the called ministers of Christ deal with us by His divine command, in particular when they exclude openly unrepentant sinners from the Christian congregation and absolve those who repent of their sins and want to do better, this is just as valid and certain, even in heaven, as if Christ our dear Lord dealt with us Himself.

Understanding the Office of the Keys

- Jesus has given to His *Church* (the body of believers) the authority to forgive the sins of those who *repent* (feel sorrow for sin and turn away from sin) and to *withhold* (not give) forgiveness from those who do not repent.

- The Office of the Keys is the authority that Jesus gave His Church to forgive sins (opening heaven) and to withhold forgiveness of sins (closing heaven).

- Christian congregations call men to serve as pastors, who publicly forgive and withhold the forgiveness of sins on behalf of the Church.

- All Christians share God's forgiveness with others in their daily lives.

> **THE MAIN IDEA**
> Jesus gives His Church the authority to forgive the sins of those who repent and to withhold forgiveness from those who refuse to repent of their sins.

Learning about the Office of the Keys

What special authority has Jesus given to His Church on earth?

Only God forgives sins through Jesus Christ. Jesus has given to His Church the authority to forgive the sins of those who repent and to withhold forgiveness from those who do not repent.

John 20:22–23   And when [Jesus] had said this, He breathed on them and said to them, "Receive the Holy Spirit. If you forgive the sins of any, they are forgiven them; if you withhold forgiveness from any, it is withheld."

Why do we call this authority the "Office of the Keys"?

Just as keys lock and unlock, the authority to forgive and withhold forgiveness of sins opens and closes heaven. Jesus gives two keys to His Church: one key forgives sins and opens heaven; the other key withholds forgiveness of sins and closes heaven to those who refuse to repent.

Matthew 16:19   I will give you the keys of the kingdom of heaven, and whatever you bind on earth shall be bound in heaven, and whatever you loose on earth shall be loosed in heaven.

Who is to be forgiven?

Everyone who repents and asks for forgiveness of their sins will be forgiven.

Psalm 32:5   I acknowledged my sin to You, and I did not cover my iniquity; I said, "I will confess my transgressions to the LORD," and You forgave the iniquity of my sin.

A Bible Illustration

Jesus gave His disciples the authority to share the forgiveness of sins that He won for the world when He died on the cross. Read about it in John 20:19–23.

How would Jesus send out the Good News of the forgiveness He won for the world?

What gave the disciples the authority to forgive and withhold forgiveness of sins?

Faith Connections

Imagine coming home from school and your older brother tells you, "I don't have the keys to the house." Ugh! It's frustrating and sometimes even dangerous when you don't have the keys to get into where you need to be.

Imagine standing outside the gates of heaven, saying, "I don't have the keys." That would be terrible!

But thanks be to God! He took care of that by sending Jesus to make a way. Jesus paid for all our sins on the cross and rose from the dead! Then He told His disciples, "I will give you the keys of the kingdom of heaven" (Matthew 16:19).

The Church has the keys! Jesus gave them to us. The Office of the Keys is the authority to forgive people in Jesus' name. When we hear God's words of forgiveness, we know God is promising the gates of heaven will swing wide open for all who believe in Jesus.

 ## Think and Share

Jesus suffered, died, and rose again to pay for the sins of the whole world. How can you share the wonderful message of Jesus' forgiveness with someone today?

 ## Sing

"As Surely as I Live," God Said (*LSB* 614:1, 5)

> "As surely as I live," God said, "I would not see the sinner dead.
> I want him turned from error's ways, Repentant, living endless days."

> The words which absolution give Are His who died that we might live;
> The minister whom Christ has sent Is but His humble instrument.

 ## Bible Memory Verse

> Receive the Holy Spirit. If you forgive the sins of any, they are forgiven them; if you withhold forgiveness from any, it is withheld. (John 20:22–23)

 ## Pray

Heavenly Father, thank You for the forgiveness of sins, won by Your Son on the cross for all people. Thank You for opening the doors of heaven to me and everyone who believes in You. In Jesus' name I pray. Amen.

Introduction to the Sacrament of the Altar

The Sacrament of the Altar is God's gift of forgiveness through the body and blood of Christ, given to believers. Jesus Himself gave us this Sacrament on the night before He was crucified.

- A sacrament is a holy act commanded by God that has an earthly element combined with God's Word and that offers the forgiveness of sins earned by Jesus Christ.
- In the Sacrament of the Altar, Christians receive the very body and blood of Jesus Christ in, with, and under the earthly elements of bread and wine.
- In the Sacrament of the Altar, we receive the forgiveness of sins won by Jesus on the cross.
- Jesus said that the bread and wine, His body and blood, are given and shed for the forgiveness of sins. We confess that the words of Jesus are powerful to do exactly what they say.
- Christians *prepare* (get ready) to receive the Sacrament of the Altar by *examining* (looking closely at) themselves and believing Jesus' promise that His body and blood are given and shed for them for the forgiveness of sins.

First

What is the Sacrament of the Altar?

It is the true body and blood of our Lord Jesus Christ under the bread and wine, instituted by Christ Himself for us Christians to eat and to drink.

Where is this written?

The holy Evangelists Matthew, Mark, Luke, and St. Paul write: Our Lord Jesus Christ, on the night when He was betrayed, took bread, and when He had given thanks, He broke it and gave it to the disciples and said: "Take, eat; this is My body, which is given for you. This do in remembrance of Me." In the same way also He took the cup after supper, and when He had given thanks, He gave it to them, saying, "Drink of it, all of you; this cup is the new testament in My blood, which is shed for you for the forgiveness of sins. This do, as often as you drink it, in remembrance of Me."

Understanding the Nature of the Sacrament of the Altar

- In the Sacrament of the Altar, we receive Jesus' true body and blood in, with, and under the bread and wine for the forgiveness of sins.

- Jesus *instituted* (began or established) the Sacrament of the Altar on the night before He went to the cross.

> **THE MAIN IDEA**
> In the Sacrament of the Altar, Christians receive the very body and blood of Jesus Christ in, with, and under the bread and wine.

Learning about the Nature of the Sacrament of the Altar

Who instituted the Sacrament of the Altar?

Jesus Christ, true God and true man, instituted this Sacrament.

1 Corinthians 11:23–24   For I received from the Lord what I also delivered to you, that the Lord Jesus on the night when He was betrayed took bread, and when He had given thanks, He broke it, and said, "This is My body, which is for you. Do this in remembrance of Me."

What does Jesus give to us in this Sacrament?

Jesus gives us His own true body and blood for the forgiveness of sins. The earthly elements Jesus uses in this Sacrament are bread and wine.

Matthew 26:26–28   Now as they were eating, Jesus took bread, and after blessing it broke it and gave it to the disciples, and said, "Take, eat; this is My body." And He took a cup, and when He had given thanks He gave it to them, saying, "Drink of it, all of you, for this is My blood of the covenant, which is poured out for many for the forgiveness of sins."

Why do we believe it is Jesus Christ's true body and His true blood in the Sacrament?

- The words "This is My body" and "This is My blood" were spoken by Jesus Christ, the very Son of God.
- God's Word teaches that in the Sacrament, the bread and wine are a *participation* (a taking part) in the body and blood of Jesus.

1 Corinthians 10:16   The cup of blessing that we bless, is it not a participation in the blood of Christ? The bread that we break, is it not a participation in the body of Christ?

Why are Jesus' words always spoken over the bread and wine by the pastor?

Without Jesus' words, this would not be a sacrament. It is by the power of Jesus' words that He gives us His body and blood in, with, and under the bread and wine.

What other names do we have for the Sacrament of the Altar?

The Sacrament of the Altar is also called the Lord's Supper, Holy Communion, and the Eucharist.

A Bible Illustration

The night before He went to the cross, Jesus instituted the Lord's Supper. Read about it in Matthew 26:17–30.

What special meal were Jesus and His disciples celebrating?

What did Jesus tell His disciples He was giving them?

Faith Connections

The night before Jesus went to the cross to pay for the sins of the world, He celebrated a special meal with His disciples. It would be the last meal that He would eat with them before He died on the cross. The special meal was called the Passover meal. The Passover meal had been celebrated for thousands of years as a way for the Israelite people to thank God and remember how He had rescued them from slavery in Egypt and had brought them to the Promised Land.

Jesus instituted the Sacrament of the Altar that night. We also call it the Lord's Supper. As Jesus gave His disciples bread and wine, He told them, "This is My body. . . . This is My blood . . . poured out for many for the forgiveness of sins" (Matthew 26:26, 28).

Christians celebrate this meal to remember how Jesus rescued us from sin and death. In this Sacrament, we receive forgiveness of sins and we look forward to the promised land of heaven that Jesus has won for us by His death and resurrection!

 ## Think and Share

What can you remember and thank Jesus for when you receive a blessing at the altar?

 ## Sing

A Blessed Feast of Highest Good (*OAR* 351:1)
> A blessed feast of highest good Has Christ Himself prepared:
> His very body and His blood With sinners freely shared.
> This ordinary wine and bread, These humble elements,
> When joined to words that Jesus said, Are made a sacrament.

 ## Bible Memory Verse

> This is My blood of the covenant, which is poured out for many for the forgiveness of sins. (Matthew 26:28)

 ## Pray

Dear Lord Jesus, thank You for the gift of forgiveness that You give to us in the Lord's Supper. Help me to remember and thank You for rescuing me from sin and death and for giving me the promise of eternal life with You in heaven. Amen.

Second

What is the benefit of this eating and drinking?
These words, "Given and shed for you for the for-giveness of sins," show us that in the Sacrament forgiveness of sins, life, and salvation are given us through these words. For where there is for-giveness of sins, there is also life and salvation.

Understanding the Benefit of the Sacrament of the Altar

- Jesus gives us a great gift in the Sacrament of the Altar: the forgiveness of sins, which He won for us by His suffering and death on the cross.

- The Sacrament of the Altar strengthens our faith and gives us life now with God and eternal life with Him in heaven.

- Jesus invites us to come often to receive this Sacrament.

> **THE MAIN IDEA**
> In the Sacrament of the Altar, we receive the forgiveness of sins won by Jesus on the cross.

Learning about the Benefit of the Sacrament of the Altar

What **benefit** *(help and blessing) is promised in the Sacrament of the Altar?*
The Sacrament of the Altar gives

- the forgiveness of sins, which Jesus won on the cross;

- life with God now as well as eternal life; and

- strengthening of our faith.

Matthew 26:28 This is My blood of the covenant, which is poured out for many for the forgiveness of sins.

John 6:40 For this is the will of My Father, that everyone who looks on the Son and believes in Him should have eternal life, and I will raise him up on the last day.

Romans 8:10 But if Christ is in you, although the body is dead because of sin, the Spirit is life because of righteousness.

Why should Christians receive the Lord's Supper often?

- Jesus invites and encourages us to receive it.

- We need the comfort and strength of Jesus' forgiveness.

- We are united with Jesus and with our fellow believers in this Sacrament.

- The Sacrament strengthens us to love and serve one another with the love of Jesus.

Matthew 26:26–28 Now as they were eating, Jesus took bread, and after blessing it broke it and gave it to the disciples, and said, "Take, eat; this is My body." And He took a cup, and when He had given thanks He gave it to them, saying, "Drink of it, all of you, for this is My blood of the covenant, which is poured out for many for the forgiveness of sins."

1 Corinthians 10:17 Because there is one bread, we who are many are one body, for we all partake of the one bread.

John 15:12 This is My commandment, that you love one another as I have loved you.

A Bible Illustration

God commanded the Israelites to eat a special meal, the Passover meal. He saved the lives of the Israelites, but He brought judgment on the Egyptians. Read about it in Exodus 12:1–14.

What did God do when He saw the blood of the lamb on the doorposts?

Why did God tell the people to celebrate the Passover year after year?

Faith Connections

What is the best gift you have ever received? What was it that made that gift so special? Maybe it was the gift itself—it was something you had been wanting for a long time or something that you really needed. Maybe it was the person who gave you that gift.

On the night before Jesus went to the cross, He gave His disciples a very special gift. It was a gift that God's people had been wanting for a very long time. It was a gift that could only come from a very special person. It was a gift that all people desperately need. This gift is the reason that Jesus came to this earth to live, suffer, die, and rise again. This gift is the forgiveness of sins that gives us new life, everlasting life with our Lord and Savior. What an incredible gift! It's the best gift.

Think and Share

Why is forgiveness of our sins such a great gift?

Sing a song, say a prayer, do a dance, or draw a picture to thank Jesus for His wonderful gift of forgiveness.

Sing

Lord Jesus Christ, You Have Prepared (*LSB* 622:1)

> Lord Jesus Christ, You have prepared This feast for our salvation;
> It is Your body and Your blood, And at Your invitation
> As weary souls, with sin oppressed, We come to You for needed rest,
> For comfort, and for pardon.

Bible Memory Verse

> But if Christ is in you, although the body is dead because of sin, the Spirit is life because of righteousness. (Romans 8:10)

Pray

Dear Jesus, You gave Your body and blood on the cross for me and for all people. Thank You for the greatest gift of all: forgiveness of my sins and life everlasting with You. Send Your Spirit to keep me close to You and strong in my faith. In Your name I pray. Amen.

Third

How can bodily eating and drinking do such great things?
Certainly not just eating and drinking do these things, but the words written here: "Given and shed for you for the forgiveness of sins." These words, along with the bodily eating and drinking, are the main thing in the Sacrament. Whoever believes these words has exactly what they say: "forgiveness of sins."

Understanding the Power of the Sacrament of the Altar

- The powerful words of Jesus, together with His body and blood in, with, and under the bread and wine, give forgiveness of sins in this Sacrament.

- Only those who believe Jesus' words that promise forgiveness in this Sacrament receive the gifts of this Sacrament.

> **THE MAIN IDEA**
> Jesus said that the bread and wine, His body and blood, are given and shed for the forgiveness of sins. We confess that the words of Jesus have the power to do exactly what they say.

Learning about the Power of the Sacrament of the Altar

How can eating and drinking the bread and wine in this Sacrament give us such great gifts?

It is not just the eating and drinking of the bread and wine, but the words of Jesus, together with His body and blood in, with, and under the bread and wine, that give forgiveness of sins.

Matthew 26:26–28 Now as they were eating, Jesus took bread, and after blessing it broke it and gave it to the disciples, and said, "Take, eat; this is My body." And He took a cup, and when He had given thanks He gave it to them, saying, "Drink of it, all of you, for this is My blood of the covenant, which is poured out for many for the forgiveness of sins."

Does everyone who eats and drinks this Sacrament receive the forgiveness of sins and eternal life?

No. Everyone who takes the Sacrament receives Jesus' body and blood. But only those who believe Jesus' words—His promise of forgiveness—receive the gifts offered in this Sacrament.

Romans 1:17   For in it the righteousness of God is revealed from faith for faith, as it is written, "The righteous shall live by faith."

A Bible Illustration

With just a few words, Jesus calmed a storm on the sea. Read about it in Mark 4:35–41.

What does this miracle tell you about the power of Jesus' words?

Think of other miracles Jesus did that show the power of His words.

Faith Connections

Our words are powerful. We can make someone smile or cause them to cry just by saying kind or hurtful words. Our words are powerful, but are they powerful enough to calm a storm? heal a person who is blind? raise a person from the dead? No way! There is only one person whose words are powerful enough to do those things: Jesus.

Jesus' words are powerful. They make things happen! So when Jesus says that the bread and wine, His body and blood, in the Lord's Supper give us the forgiveness of sins, we believe Him! Jesus' words have the power to do exactly what they say.

 ## Think and Share

Give an example of how Jesus' words are powerful.

What are some of your favorite words and promises of Jesus? Why are they so important and special to you? (Here are some you might want to look up: John 11:25; Matthew 11:28; John 14:6; John 3:16.)

 ## Sing

A Blessed Feast of Highest Good (*OAR* 351:2)
> "This is My body, take and eat; Take, drink, this is My blood."
> Our Savior's words we thus repeat To consecrate this food.
> So Jesus gives Himself to us In this most Holy Meal,
> In ways unseen, mysterious, By eyes of faith revealed.

 ## Bible Memory Verse

For in it the righteousness of God is revealed from faith for faith, as it is written, "The righteous shall live by faith." (Romans 1:17)

 ## Pray

Dear Lord Jesus, Your words are powerful! You calmed storms, healed the sick, and raised the dead. I know that Your words do what they say. Thank You for promising the forgiveness of sins in the Sacrament of the Altar. Help me always to trust in You and in Your Word. In Your name I pray. Amen.

Fourth

Who receives this sacrament worthily?
Fasting and bodily preparation are certainly fine outward training. But that person is truly worthy and well prepared who has faith in these words: "Given and shed for you for the forgiveness of sins."

But anyone who does not believe these words or doubts them is unworthy and unprepared, for the words "for you" require all hearts to believe.

Understanding How to Receive This Sacrament Worthily

- We should *examine* (look closely at) ourselves for our sinfulness before receiving the Sacrament of the Altar.

- We are *prepared* (ready) to receive the Lord's Supper when we believe we are sinners, when we repent of our sins, when we believe in Jesus and His words of promise in the Sacrament, and when we plan to live a new life pleasing to God with the help of the Holy Spirit.

> **THE MAIN IDEA**
> Christians prepare to receive the Sacrament of the Altar by examining themselves and believing Jesus' promise that His body and blood are given and shed for them for the forgiveness of sins.

- Jesus welcomes those who are weak or struggling in the faith to receive the Sacrament for the strengthening of their faith.

Learning about How to Receive This Sacrament Worthily

How are we to examine ourselves before receiving the Sacrament of the Altar?
We should

- admit we have sinned and be sorry for our sins;

- believe in our Savior, Jesus Christ, and in His words in the Sacrament; and

- with the help of the Holy Spirit, plan to live a new life that is pleasing to God.

Psalm 38:18   I confess my iniquity; I am sorry for my sin.

Luke 22:19–20   And He took bread, and when He had given thanks, He broke it and gave it to them, saying, "This is My body, which is given for you. Do this in remembrance of Me." And likewise the cup after they had eaten, saying, "This cup that is poured out for you is the new covenant in My blood."

Ephesians 4:22–24   To put off your old self, which belongs to your former manner of life and is corrupt through deceitful desires, and to be renewed in the spirit of your minds, and to put on the new self, created after the likeness of God in true righteousness and holiness.

Who should not be given the Sacrament?

- Those who are not Christian or who are not baptized.
- Christians who have a different confession of faith, since the Lord's Supper is an outward sign of our unity in faith and *doctrine* (what we teach and believe).

Acts 2:42   And they devoted themselves to the apostles' teaching and the fellowship, to the breaking of bread and the prayers.

May believers who feel weak in faith come to the Sacrament?

Yes! Jesus welcomes weak and struggling believers to the Sacrament in order to strengthen their faith in Him.

John 6:37   All that the Father gives Me will come to Me, and whoever comes to Me I will never cast out.

Mark 9:24   Immediately the father of the child cried out and said, "I believe; help my unbelief!"

A Bible Illustration

St. Paul tells us that we should think about what we believe before going to the Lord's Supper. Read it in 1 Corinthians 11:23–28.

Jesus said that we take His true body and true blood with the bread and wine in the Lord's Supper. How important is it to believe Jesus' words?

Why would it be foolish to doubt or disbelieve Jesus' words?

Faith Connections

Do you like taking tests? St. Paul tells us that we should test ourselves before taking the Lord's Supper. But don't worry—in the Bible, God tells us everything we need to know for this test, and He gives us His Holy Spirit to help us. Here are some of the questions that we should ask ourselves before taking the Lord's Supper:

Do you believe that you are a sinner? Are you sorry for your sins? Do you believe that Jesus is your Savior? Do you want to live a better life with the help of the Holy Spirit? Do you believe that Jesus gives us His true body and true blood in, with, and under the bread and wine? Do you believe that Jesus promises the forgiveness of sins in the Sacrament of the Altar?

God wants to give us His good gifts. He prepares us for the Lord's Supper by making us His children in Baptism, giving us His Word, and sending His Spirit so that we know His truth. What a loving God we have!

Think and Share

What is one question a person might ask him- or herself before going to the Sacrament of the Altar?

Sing

A Blessed Feast of Highest Good (*OAR* 351:3)
> Come, penitent, and be assured Of pardon, life made new.
> How worthy those who trust His word: "Here giv'n and shed for you."
> Come to the Table of His grace; Forgiveness here is found.
> Life and salvation here we taste, And heav'nly joys abound.

Bible Memory Verse

Put on the new self, created after the likeness of God in true righteousness and holiness. (Ephesians 4:24)

Pray

Lord Jesus, I confess that I am sinful and I need Your forgiveness. I believe that You are my Lord and Savior, who died and rose for me. Thank You for the gifts of forgiveness and eternal life that You give in the Lord's Supper. Send Your Holy Spirit to help me live a life that is pleasing to You. In Your name I pray. Amen.

Table of Duties

Bible verses that tell us what we should be doing in our daily lives and vocations, or callings (the positions and jobs that God has given us to do).

Of Citizens

1 Timothy 2:1–3   I urge that supplications, prayers, intercessions, and thanksgivings be made for all people, for kings and all who are in high positions, that we may lead a peaceful and quiet life, godly and dignified in every way. This is good, and it is pleasing in the sight of God our Savior.

Titus 3:1   Remind them to be submissive to rulers and authorities, to be obedient, to be ready for every good work.

To Parents

Ephesians 6:4   Fathers, do not provoke your children to anger, but bring them up in the discipline and instruction of the Lord.

To Children

Ephesians 6:1–3   Children, obey your parents in the Lord, for this is right. "Honor your father and mother" (this is the first commandment with a promise), "that it may go well with you and that you may live long in the land."

To Youth

1 Peter 5:5–6   Likewise, you who are younger, be subject to the elders. Clothe yourselves, all of you, with humility toward one another, for "God opposes the proud but gives grace to the humble." Humble yourselves, therefore, under the mighty hand of God so that at the proper time He may exalt you.

To Everyone

Romans 13:9   For the commandments, "You shall not commit adultery, You shall not murder, You shall not steal, You shall not covet," and any other commandment, are summed up in this word: "You shall love your neighbor as yourself."

Let each his lesson learn with care,
And all the household well share fare.

Catechism Glossary

Absolution The pastor's announcement of the forgiveness of sins.

absolve To forgive sins.

adultery When a person desires or has sexual relations with someone to whom he or she is not married.

amen A Hebrew word that means "so shall it be." We are certain God hears our prayers.

angel A spirit created by God to serve Him.

anoint To apply oil on a person or thing to set apart as holy.

atone To make up for a wrong that has been done.

atonement Payment for sin.

authorities Those who have the right to tell us what to do and the responsibility to watch over us.

Baptism A sacrament in which God forgives our sins through water and His Word.

begotten Brought into existence by a parent.

bless To give good things to; to honor as holy.

blessing Special favor or good things from God.

called Invited or brought into God's service.

catechism A book explaining the basic teachings of the Christian faith.

Christ A Greek title for Jesus meaning "the Anointed One."

Christian A person who professes faith in Jesus Christ.

commitment Dedication to a person or cause.

Communion Another name for the Sacrament of the Altar; a joining or coming together.

conception The moment at which life begins.

confess To admit to having done wrong; to state what you believe.

confession The act of admitting guilt; a statement of faith.

Confirmation A rite of the church in which an instructed Christian makes a public confession of faith and pledges faithfulness to Christ.

contrition The feeling and expression of sadness about one's sins.

covenant A formal agreement between individuals or groups in which one or both sides agree to fulfill a promise; a special agreement God made with His people.

covet A sinful desire to have or to take away something that belongs to someone else.

creature Any living being made by God.

creed A summary of beliefs.

deliver To rescue or set free.

despise To be disrespectful toward or to view as unimportant.

devil A fallen angel who fights against God and tempts us to sin.

disciple A student who learns from a teacher; a follower of Jesus.

Divine Service Worship service that often includes the celebration of the Lord's Supper.

doctrine A teaching.

entice To coax or cause to come away.

eternal Without beginning or end; forever.

evil Sinful; the force of things that are bad.

faith Belief and trust in God and His promises; trust in a person or concept.

faithful Loyal to a person or cause.

faithfulness Remaining true to a commitment.

flesh The physical body with natural desires; our sinful way of thinking and acting.

forgive To pardon a wrong or sin.

glory Wonderful beauty and majesty; praise, honor.

gods Things or figures people love and trust to take care of their needs; not the true God.

Gospel The Good News that Jesus died to pay for our sins and rose; through faith in Him we have eternal life.

grace God's undeserved favor toward sinners.

guilt Responsibility for doing wrong; feelings of deserving blame.

hallowed Holy, sacred, without sin.

holy Set apart; sacred; pure, without sin.

honor To highly regard in thought, speech, and action.

humility State of lowliness; opposite of being proud.

hymn Song of prayer or praise, usually in stanza form.

idol A false god; an object that is worshiped.

idolatry Worshiping a false god.

incarnation The event in which the Son of God became man.

iniquity Sin; wickedness.

institute To begin or establish.

intercede To speak for someone else; to pray to God for the needs of another person.

judge One who decides who is right or wrong; to blame, condemn.

justified To be made right with God through faith in Jesus, who took the punishment for our sins.

kingdom of God God's rule over His people and His creation.

Law All the rules given by God to His people; the Law shows us our sin.

marriage A legally binding commitment between a man and a woman.

Means of Grace The written and spoken Word of the Gospel and the Sacraments of Baptism and Holy Communion. These are the ways or means by which God gives us the forgiveness, life, and salvation won by the death and resurrection of Jesus Christ.

meditate To think prayerfully; to ponder and reflect on.

Messiah A Hebrew title for Jesus meaning "the Anointed One."

neighbor Any and every person.

obedience The act of doing the will of another.

old Adam Our sinful self that we inherited because of Adam's fall into sin.

Passover Annual festival held in remembrance of God's deliverance in Egypt when the angel of death spared the firstborn of those whose houses were marked with the blood of a lamb.

peace A calmness and sense of being at rest.

petition A specific prayer or request.

proceeding Coming forth from or coming out of.

profane To show dishonor or disrespect to God's name or to religious teaching.

prophecy A message of truth from God, given through a person.

prophet One who speaks a message from God.

redeem To save, rescue, or buy back.

redemption Deliverance from sin; salvation.

repent To change; to turn away from sin.

repentance A turning away from sin to faith in Jesus and His forgiveness.

respect To honor or hold in high regard.

resurrection Coming to life after being dead.

Sabbath The seventh day of the week; the day set aside for rest and worship.

sacred Holy, blessed by God; set apart for a special purpose.

sacrifice To give up something of value for someone else's benefit.

saints Believers, Christians; people who have been sanctified by God.

salvation Deliverance from the power of sin and death. God's free gift of eternal life through faith in Jesus Christ.

sanctification All of the Holy Spirit's work in the lives of believers, from calling them by the Gospel to raising them to life on the Last Day; spiritual growth throughout the life of a Christian.

sanctify To make holy; set apart for service to God.

Satan The devil. The name *Satan* means "enemy."

Scripture The written words of God, the Bible.

sin Wrongs; evil; to do the opposite of God's will and commands.

sinful nature Our natural desire to disobey God.

slander To say something false and hurtful about someone.

soul A person's spiritual nature, which lives forever.

spiritual Having to do with the spirit and soul.

sponsors Individuals who serve as witnesses to a Baptism, pray for the baptized child, and help raise the child in the Christian faith. Sponsors are also called godparents.

supplication Prayer that asks God for something.

tempt To encourage a person to sin.

temptation A strong feeling to do something wrong.

testimony A statement of something as fact.

transgression A wrongdoing or sin.

trespass To cross a boundary; a serious wrongdoing; sin.

triune Three in one.

trust To rely upon or place hope in.

victory Success in defeating an enemy; win.

vocation A person's calling or position in life; includes our work or careers as well as our relationships with God and others (child of God, son, daughter, father, husband, wife, and so on).

witness To give an account of what has been seen and heard; to state what one believes.

worship To show praise and honor to God; a ceremony of praise and honor.

worthy Acceptable or qualified.

The Apostles' Creed

I believe in God, the Father Almighty, Maker of heaven and earth.

And in Jesus Christ, His only Son, our Lord, who was conceived by the Holy Spirit, born of the Virgin Mary, suffered under Pontius Pilate, was crucified, died and was buried. He descended into hell. The third day He rose again from the dead. He ascended into heaven and sits at the right hand of God, the Father Almighty. From thence He will come to judge the living and the dead.

I believe in the Holy Spirit, the holy Christian church, the communion of saints, the forgiveness of sins, the resurrection of the body, and the life everlasting. Amen.

The Lord's Prayer

Our Father who art in heaven, hallowed be Thy name, Thy kingdom come, Thy will be done on earth as it is in heaven. Give us this day our daily bread; and forgive us our trespasses as we forgive those who trespass against us; and lead us not into temptation, but deliver us from evil. For Thine is the kingdom and the power and the glory forever and ever. Amen.